# EAT TO LOVE..

## Sweet Bites for the Mouth & Heart

By W. Kay Wilson

Copyright ©2014

Photograph copyright ©2014 by JehanDaughertyPhoto

Library of Congress

Wilson, W.Kay

EAT TO LOVE..sweet bites for the mouth and heart/ by W. Kay Wilson

ISBN 978-0-692-23503-4

Summary: 1. Cookery, African American 2. Relationships 3. Wilson, W.Kay Anecdotes

Also by author: "Holding On To Somewhere" by W. Kay (Shabazz) Wilson- Provided by Publisher Carbon2Diamond Press  ISBN: 978-0-615-43567-1 ISBN 10: 061543567X

Publisher website address: www.Carbon2DiamondPress.com

Cover design by: Adriel Harris

# DEDICATIONS

This book is dedicated to my lion & my panther; Marcus & Stokley-I pray you success & joy. You were given this life because God knows you are strong enough to LIVE it. I love you. I am so proud and so grateful that God chose me to be your mom. To my bonus kids; Ashely, Karliah, Karlil & grand babes- Ja'Leah & Ja'Shay thank you for adding to my life. My husband, KP-I adore your strength & your heart for God. K2W for always!

My 10 to win: Julie M, Dorian H, Laura C, Yvonne C, Kaneeka P, Trenia D, Adriel H, Pam L, Tanya L, & Roshanda- Thank you for your encouraging phone calls, spontaneous laughs in the kitchen & your discerning taste buds.

PREHEAT * 1

*INGREDIENT DEVIANT * 9*

KITCHEN VIXEN * 11

NOURISH A MAN, MARINATE A WOMAN * 15

GOIN' FISHIN' * 25

*DISH ON FISH * 31*

WHEN TO SAY WHEN: LEFT OVERS & DO OVERS * 41

*SAMMIES & WIENERS * 53*

ONE MAN'S STORY ANOTHER WOMAN'S STEW * 65

*JERKS, CHICKENS, MEATLOAFS & LIMP NOODLES * 71*

GOOD INGREDIENTS VS. FANCY PACKAGING * 81

*CROCK POT & VEGGIE MEALS * 91*

'MAN' THE KITCHEN THIS LADY 'BURNS' * 137

*HOW TO MAKE MENUS * 141*

THE FLAVOR OF FAVOR: SWEET & SOUR * 189

*Mo' BETTA SUBSTITUTES * 197*

THE HONEY & THE MONEY * 203

*CAKES, SWEETS, THE ULTIMATE COOKIE & GOOD NUTS * 209*

**MISE EN PLACE**: (mi za plas) –n French. (in a professional kitchen) meaning "putting in place" getting tools & ingredients together

A note to all who are reading this; I love you and I honor you. You didn't do anything wrong. There are times when the best students get the hardest tests. When God has something for you to do -hen He has a gift for you- He will test you to be sure you are ready.

This may feel familiar. You're sitting on your couch, eating one of your favorite comfort snacks, watching television. Suddenly, the leading man is in the midst of a romantic '*I'm so into you, no one gets to me like you do, you changed me and make me break my own rules*' speech, and you're awe struck. Not able to take another bite, you hang onto his every word. I suppose women in movie audiences or living rooms across the globe get so touched by these wildly improbable scenes because they also feel that what they have is an exception to the rules. I used to be one of those women, even though I knew the odds made it unlikely. It didn't matter how much love I gave or how supportive I was, it takes two people to make a commitment. I couldn't be the exception for someone who wasn't for me. You can't be either.

I take a ridiculous pleasure in what I eat and drink. I find that the table is one of the most intimate places in our lives because you can see how we give ourselves to one another. When we say, *Take some more, let me serve you another plate, let me pour you another glass, how do you like it?* We say much more than words express.

People bond over a meal because it's tied to the power food has to nourish and sustain our bodies, as well as the way it allows us to make compelling symbolic associations embedded in thoughts of comfort and home. At some level, we all understand the language of food.

There is a magnetism that takes place when people share a meal together. The energy will either repel or connect. In my opinion, this makes it all the more important that the food we serve each other be good, tasty food that will nourish us - body and soul.

My prayer is that this book will help open your heart, your eyes and your taste-buds. The table is set and you're not alone. Use this as a guide to improve a discerning palette for what you have on the table or across the table. There is power in the tongue, with the words we speak and the food we receive.

The mouth holds great command and to a large extent can determine the kind of life that we will create for ourselves. The term when we know better, we do better, should apply to our relationship with ourselves, and with others. You should know you deserve as much love and attention as you would give to anyone else.

Many people are aware that your mood can kill your appetite, trigger food cravings or cause you to overeat. However, were you aware that the food you eat can make or break your mood? This is apparent shortly after you've eaten, but over time, what you eat helps to shape your mental health from the inside out. Good food and exercise can help you reduce stress and help you be nicer to others. I find Zumba and weight training helps me. If you feel better, you're a better partner and you're less vulnerable to stress.

Dr. Joseph Mercola, osteopathic specialist and alternative medicine proponent declared in his 2011 Huffington Post article, "I simply cannot overstate the importance of your food choices when it comes to your mental health. In a very real sense, you have TWO brains-one in your head, and one in your gut-both of which are created from the same tissue during fetal development.

These two systems are connected via your vagus nerve, the tenth cranial nerve that runs from your brain stem down to your abdomen. It is now well established that the vagus nerve is the primary route your gut bacteria uses to transmit information to your brain."

Relationships and recipes are about putting the right qualities of information together. As an example, think about baking. In general, baking ingredients can be divided into two categories; 'tougheners' or strengtheners, (ex: flour, eggs) and tenderizers or weakeners (ex. Fats, sugars). In order for a recipe to bake with all of the qualities we enjoy, like being tender, fluffy, moist, chewy and tasty, there needs to be the proper balance between the two categories. If one is increased, the other should be decreased, but they need to be mixed in the proper quantities.

Recipes vary by the amounts of each ingredient and the mixing techniques used to combine them. The amount of heat applied and the length of time it needs to cook also affects the final baked product. Each ingredient in a recipe contributes to the taste of the final baked good. Each experience or value system in a person contributes to the way they relate to other people. The combination creates a substance (product or person) that can both change its shape (or perspective) and ability to bounce back.

While making bread the dough can change its shape, but it resists the change and tries to form back to its original shape. I have been a dough girl, often going back to familiar actions, rather than learning from previous errors and making necessary changes for better results. The flour and water forms the network that gives bread its shape. Adding shortening and butter will make the dough more workable, giving the final product moistness and flavor. Our strengthener is our belief system and our tenderizers are the bad past experiences through which we've lived. What we bring into our relationships is a combination of both and we can present ourselves as tasty or sour.

Think of this book as the eggs, which are binders to help hold all of the ingredients together. Egg whites are often used to produce a light airy texture, while yolks contribute to the color, flavor, and texture of baked goods. Let's say you want to make a reduced fat cake. The number of egg whites you choose to use can be adjusted, but too many will make your cake dry. Some of the suggestions and examples will be familiar to you, but how much you take and what you use are up to you.

I learned how to cook from my Grandmother and bake from my mom. It was countless hours of experimenting in the kitchen, of my own restaurant, that solidified my level of comfort in the kitchen. So when I plan a meal, I start with the foundation I know, use the techniques I've learned and take some chances. This is the same approach you should take in finding your ideal relationship. There isn't a fool- proof recipe.

Recipes are guidelines. You can only know its right to your own taste. These pages are guidelines. There is no real instruction on finding 'the one'. If you are asking whether or not you've found *the one* then you are confused about the equation. *Are they the one for what; the one for now, the one for this time, the one to be with, the one to teach, the one to learn from, the one to heal with, the one* **for what**?

It doesn't matter whether you learned to cook from your mother, grandmother, uncle or on your own. Nor does it matter from where you gained your experience. You can use what you know and take some chances, pick up a couple of things to add spice to your life, and likely get good results.

You have to be brave and a little creative, but if you are reading this book, you are probably both. Some people have told me they read cookbooks like novels. I suspect they do so as much to get ideas as to get specific recipes. As you read, you become more self-aware. This will lead to better decisions. Continual learning puts you in a better position to get the results you want.

I don't know many people who meticulously collect and measure exactly all of the specific ingredients required in a recipe, and I don't expect anyone to follow this book to the page either. Your personality may be fed through structure-following a recipe and continually practicing it to memory may be your style. Variety could be the spice of your life-make changes to excite your taste buds. Digest the information within these pages to your own taste. The moment you stop trying to please everyone else's tastes and learn what savors you enjoy, you will become a great cook. The minute we stop trying to find the right mate, and started trying to *become* the right mate...the companion will come.

In recipes and relationships you need to learn to trust yourself. Next time a recipe seems weird to you, it probably is. Trust yourself and move on! Being mindful can heal a broken relationship with people or with food.

# PREHEAT

If you want to be the best judge of character, you need to be tutored by the one who creates each and every character. Start with God. You should study His word long enough to be near to Him before you try to get near someone else. God is love. Love is always present; teaching, guiding and growing us. All relationships are of benefit to the growth of our soul. They all contain lessons which we are here to learn. No relationship is a mistake if you have learned something...and moved on. Life will throw you bricks, but each one will go to help you build a stronger foundation.

Good recipes will ask you to preheat your oven before you actually start any of the preparation. Allowing your oven time to reach the correct temperature before you put anything in it, is possibly the single most important thing you can do when you are cooking. Food cooks unevenly when an oven is cold. If you don't preheat your oven, the temperature may not be hot enough and the end result could be a heavy, undercooked mess.

The same applies when planning to get into the dating game. It's going to take a little time and a bit of heat. The hottest thing you can do when you are ready to get out and date has nothing to do with purchasing a new push up bra or an appointment with the hairdresser. Knowing if you are ready entails deep moments of self-reflection regarding your beliefs, attitudes and behaviors in a real, open and honest way. This part is never easy.

If you find that you're often trying to change something about yourself, thinking it will make you more attractive to the person you just met, then you are, lacking confidence in yourself. We have all been there. Don't be too hard on yourself, this is common, but it means that you need to work on finding and loving the real you before trying to love someone else.

Women are used to putting on accessories and make-up to hide flaws. This makes it easy to understand how women could easily transfer their real beauty to hide behind masks and emotional armor. They deny, obstruct, and cover their pain because they are beholden to the opinions and personas of others.

The pain they feel will transfer onto other women they teach, lead, and coach because they themselves are broken, and broken people break things!

Sometimes our mind finds it hard to accept that regardless of how hard, challenging or scary an experience may seem, everything you went through was necessary in order for us to learn, grow and prepare for who we need to be. If we want to let go and be free of the anger, shame or heaviness we have felt from feeling like the relationship failure was ours, or that someone must have thought we weren't enough, if we want to be valued, we have to practice some level of vulnerability.

Accepting what happened doesn't mean you appreciate, agree with, or overlook what someone may have done to you. It means you realize, regardless of what happened, that it didn't happen *to you*. It happened *for you*. Holding onto judgment is blocking your chances of finding your match, because you will always be setting yourself up to be judged. If someone cheated on you, the lesson you experienced was not for you to trust them. It was to teach you to trust yourself. The lesson is meant for you to learn and become better, not bitter. The best thing you can do for your new relationship is to stop believing that there is anything wrong with the way your old relationships ended. Vulnerability in love means taking emotional risks. Are you willing to take a chance waking up every day and loving someone who may or may not love us back, whose safety we can't ensure, who may stay in our lives or may leave without a moment's notice, who may be loyal to the day they die or betray us tomorrow?

Convinced that the other shoe may drop at any moment, you will lay in wait for an indication that your new date is untrustworthy and has shadowy motives behind *too good to be true* gestures, or erratic behavior. Since no one is perfect, you will manage to piece together *evidence* that the new date is guilty of disappointments and deception. If you adopt a zero tolerance policy or won't give him the benefit of the doubt when he shows any indication of your ex's old patterns, you will get what you expect.

Despite his commitment or desire, eventually, 'the new guy' will begin to feel like there isn't any point in continuing to make the effort since he feels that in your mind, he is guilty until proven innocent, and your attachment to seeing him that way will make the possibility of seeing his innocence remote at best.

Your attachment to your judgments prevents you from appreciating everything he brings to the table. Although you have a right to feel hurt, staying there puts the deterioration of the relationship on your table. If you continue to focus on the other person's part in the breakdown it will make it hard for you to recognize the part that you play, and consequently prevent you from seeing what you could do to make the relationship work.

When we bring old judgments onto new people we are letting them know right away that there are conditions to our loving them. New people are in the dark to our past pain. People who are walking in the dark are fearful. When they are afraid, they feel powerless and look for a sense of control. They can't control when you leave, but they can decide when they will leave.

When he eventually tells you he is no longer willing to keep trying to prove his adoration, you will take this this as more "proof" that he's 'just like the rest' and didn't really care. Next time you are on a date try to keep an open mind, at least for the duration of the date. It may help to withhold judgment until after the date is over, preferably until the next day when you have had a chance to reflect on whether it is mismatched values or judgment. This will stop you from assessing everything your date does or doesn't do and judging their suitability moment by moment. Trust your heart rather than your head; it is usually far more discerning and less judgmental. Ultimately judgments will prevent you both from experiencing a satisfying and fulfilling connection together.

I don't recall ever feeling resentful of any of my married friends because it's not like they married MY husband. Who God had for me was going to be for me. I just needed to wait on God-which history could reveal, I have not always been obedient or patient.

It's always better to communicate your boundaries up front than to build one after someone has crossed a line he couldn't see and of which he wasn't aware. In the beginning you can ask for what you want without months or years of built-up resentment and anger being the water under your bridge. You're simply showing a new individual your standards. Don't be afraid to speak up. A solid, safe person will respect your limits.

The next step is to *be* who you want to attract. If you want to attract a positive, open, honest, healthy and trustworthy person, then from the depths of all that you are, on every level (mental, emotional, spiritual, and physical) strive your hardest to be all of those things that you want to attract in someone else. Being yourself is the best way for you attract the type of person you want. Relationships are like magnets in that way. If you are a negative thinker, a critical person, then you will find yourself attracting others who will reinforce your negative belief system. If you are a woman who thinks all men are dogs, then you will continue to attract more men who are dogs to reinforce your belief about men. If you serendipitously happen to bump in to a great guy, you will probably send him running in the opposite direction with the defensive energy you are projecting. If you have baggage, such as trust issues and emotional scars, take the time to find balance and deal with those issues so you can find balance and healing. Wounded people generally only attract wounded people. Don't ever go into dating thinking someone else is ever going to fix you or fix your life. Only you can do that for you. Dating will only serve as a distraction to dealing with your issues.

If you are on the other end of the spectrum and feel you are fine with who you are, but everyone you date seems to have an issue. Keep this in mind: All relationships are mirrors, reflecting back to us different aspects of ourselves, helping us to see what we cannot see on our own. Sometimes they reflect back to us a beautiful image and sometimes an ugly image. If you don't like what you see in your partner (mirror), then you need to look in the mirror and ask yourself what aspect of me is this person reflecting back to me? If you are willing to do this, without ego and denial getting in the way, then you may bring light to a dysfunctional pattern that exists in your past relationships. I am not implying that anyone deserves to be hurt physically-ever, (my last book, *HOLDING ON TO SOMEWHERE* shares an experience with abuse) or emotionally. You have to ask yourself what you are reflecting. In my own case, I saw warning signs, but I was in the way of both of us learning the lesson God had in mind.

It's just a date! A date is like an extended audition. You can't start by asking yourself; "Will this be my spouse?" When we're dating, we often look for people who are mirror images of who we believe we are. Look for someone who compliments you, not competes with you. Don't look for an 'upgrade' from where you are and have it be to your own detriment. Having a fantasy is good fun, but it can set you up for failure. Don't come to a date with a sack load of expectations that you're ready to throw down on some poor, unsuspecting bum. Don't fail to take an honest look at yourself or the date. Someone can seem like your knight in shining armor only because you're wearing your knight-in-shining-armor shades. I have guy friends who have shades too. They call them beer goggles or swimming pool shades (thanks Kendrick Lamar). If someone seems too good to be true, they could be. If they are good, time will tell. Stay sober, literally and metaphorically, so you can see people for who they really are. Don't move to get 'drunk in love' and cause an accident.

My girlfriends and I have talked about how we've often been embarrassed by the way we have dismissed guys, often sight unseen, evaluating them as being too-something or not-something enough. I listen as they laugh about the stories in their twenties when guys were falling over themselves to get their numbers. Each of us giggles as we remember the false *club* names we would use to throw guys off of our tracks. Now that we are older we've discovered it's not that the available men who are our age aren't datable-as many single women complain. It's just that they don't appear like the person we've imagined being with since we were in our twenties. Isn't the goal to marry someone you love deeply, which is going to make you happy and treat you well? Where in that sentence does it talk about his six pack, real estate square footage, or car model—all the things girls perceive reflects their own image.

Millennials and others, who are more comfortable dating on sites such as Grouper, might say modern love is a group sport. And the arena is the entire Internet. These thoughts are coming from an upcoming generation that is growing up receiving trophies for their participation. Dating is for gladiators; and gladiators don't do what is comfortable. They do what is courageous. The choice you make to date is one of comfort or courage – because these are mutually exclusive; there is nothing comfortable in courage. If you go into that arena you may get booed and you may get your ass kicked, but you get into the arena.

Dating is pairing off to experience the kind of one-on-one association that encourages conversation. Grouping doesn't allow you to see how you will be treated in a one-on-one situation. Dating gives opportunities to learn how to initiate and sustain a mature relationship. Having courage to push through rejection can also strengthen life skills outside of personal relationships. None of that happens when you go out with a group. I love my crew, but some of them can't commit to a cell phone contract, work- out schedule, or weekly Bible study- so I know better than to bring them into any area I am committing to.

Save girls night for shopping, not dating. I'm sure we all have many friends who love to shop in groups, but shopping is not like dating. In shopping no one is pointing out the shopper's own flaws. How often do we show our vulnerability in our own bad choices?

Using guerilla tactics for dating seemed crazy after I reflected on it. We don't subject other important aspects of our lives to pure chance and group opinion. When you are looking for a job, you don't hang out in lobbies, hoping an employer will stop and start talking with you. When you want to buy a house, you don't walk neighborhood to neighborhood, aimlessly hoping to spot a house that happens to be for sale, contains the right number of bedrooms, has the appropriate kitchen accommodations, and has a spa-sized bathtub? You certainly wouldn't do it with a group, like a neighborhood block-watch. If you did, you would find yourself homeless for a while. You hire a real estate broker, or in the least, go onto the internet to see potential homes that meet your needs. By the same token, why wouldn't you sit down and write out what you want in a potential partner?

I have friends who say they want to settle down, but they spend time weighing their options, always keeping one guy in the wings. That's cool-but I am not made up that way. It's insane to go through post-date- play by play each week with girlfriends, reassuring them that there is nothing wrong with them, that the guy was a dork, only to have them spew the same bland reassurance to me the following weekend after my own dating shenanigans. It was a disappointing waste of the precious time God gave us on the Earth, going through a string of temporary encounters when we could be building a lifetime of shared memories and experiences in a committed relationship with one person. I don't care to spend my time analyzing phone messages, emails, body language, wasting hours over dinners or the movies with a guy who will be out of the picture in a few days or a few months, only to be replaced by what's behind door number two.

When you have children- your list of needs compounds or even changes. Of course you want to share the little moments of your child's life with someone who cares about them as profoundly as you do, but you also have to be protective of them as well. Don't get me wrong, I am not saying being in a relationship if you have a child is a requirement for survival. I am speaking to those who have the desire to be in a relationship.

We all know the idea of looking across the room and locking eyes with a random stranger seems more appealing, but in which rooms are you going to find this stranger? Your office? Giant Eagle? At the gym? Maybe at a club? This is not the best place to find high-quality men.

If you are like many of my single sisters, who "*Lean In*" (Sheryl Sandberg) during the week at the office, lean back when you can catch an episode of *Scandal* or chat with girlfriends, lean over when you are at the gym or cleaning up the house & lean on while you are at your place of worship, you don't have much time left to lock eyes with anyone. I'm not saying it can't happen, but do you want to continue to leave things up to fate or destiny?

You *could* take another option;

A store has just opened downtown that offers free husbands, but when women go to choose a husband, they have to read and follow the instructions at the entrance:

**"You may visit this store ONLY ONCE! There are six floors from which you may choose. You may choose any item from a particular floor, or you may choose to go up to the next floor, but you CANNOT go back down except to exit the building!"**

So, a woman goes to the store to find a husband. She gets to the first floor. The sign on the door reads: Floor 1- **These men Have Jobs**

The 2nd floor sign reads: Floor 2 -**These men Have Jobs and Love Kids**.

The 3rd floor sign reads: Floor 3- **These men Have Jobs, Love Kids and are extremely Handsome.** "Wow," she thinks, but feels compelled to keep going. She goes to the 4th floor and sign reads:

Floor 4- **These men Have Jobs, Love Kids, are Drop-dead Good Looking and Help with Housework.**"This is bananas!" she exclaims. "I can hardly stand it!" Still, she goes to the 5th floor and sign reads:

Floor 5- **These men Have Jobs, love Kids, are Drop-dead Gorgeous, help with Housework and are impulsive romantics.** She is so tempted to stay, but she goes to the 6th floor and the Sign reads:

Floor 6 -**You are visitor 71,456,012 to this floor. There are no men on this floor. This floor exists solely as proof that you are impossible to please.**

*Thank you for shopping at the Husband Store.*

To avoid gender bias charges, the store's owner opened a *Wife Store* just across the street. The 1st first floor **has wives that love sex**.

The 2nd floor has wives that **love sex and are caring**.

The 3rd floor has **wives that love sex, are caring and love to watch sports**.

The 4th through 6th floors have never been visited....

*My version* of an old joke...

    *So,* I started with **me**. Let's start by writing down all the reasons a potential partner *wouldn't* want to date *me*- all the things they would have to put up with if they chose to be with *me*.

# *INGREDIENT DEVIANT*

- Fat is easiest to decrease in baked goods that use oil. Start by replacing half the oil with unsweetened applesauce. If you like the final product, use more applesauce and less oil. If you find it too dry or dissimilar from the original, add back some oil.

- Certified Organic Grass-Fed Butter should be substituted for shortening or margarine in any recipe.

- Raw granulated sugar may be substituted for white sugar in any recipe. Stevia may be used in any recipe that does not require the "sugar" to caramelize.

- An egg may be omitted if you add 1 Tablespoon Almond milk powder, 1 Tablespoon Cornstarch and 2 Tablespoon Water to any baked good or 1 tablespoon flax meal (first) plus 3 tablespoons water, refrigerate for 20 minutes.

- An egg may be omitted if you add ½ ripe banana mashed.

- Adding nut butter or fiber reduces the glycemic index of a food.

- Aluminum free baking powder should be used in place of the traditional grocery store brands.

- Baking powder combined with sour or butter milk makes a nice leavening.

- Carob chips or organic chocolate chips may be substituted in any recipe that requires chocolate chips.

- Vanilla may be made by soaking 2 vanilla beans (broken into 1" pieces) in a pint of vodka or rum for 6 weeks.

# *KITCHEN VIXEN*

Many of my friends often tell me they can't cook with the same frustration they have in not finding any 'good' men. After we have a conversation I find out that cooking is rarely the problem. The problem is the frustration of not having what they need when it's time to cook. You know the dilemma, cereal with no milk, peanut butter, no jelly. If you stock your kitchen with healthy items that you can throw together for a meal, your family is much more likely to eat healthfully, as well as spend less money on convenience foods and eating out.

I have been paid to be a grocery consultant in the past- I know it seems ridiculous, but I have had people give me the address of the grocery store they shop at most frequently and I 'map out' their shopping route and list in order to help them save time and money and take the stress out of their meal-planning experience; now most local stores have aps to help ease your shopping experience.

I went through my pantry this weekend in hopes to help people out with what they should stock in their kitchen. Regarding where all the good men are; we'll talk about that later.

Try to buy local (for every mile your food travels it loses micronutrients) and locate produce that has been organically grown by choosing PLUs that start with 9. This guarantees that you are not eating Genetically Modified Organisms.

*BAD:* Four- digit codes starting with 3 or 4 (grown with pesticides & chemicals)

*BAD:* Five-digit codes starting with an 8 (grown genetically modified)

*GOOD:* Five-digit codes starting with a 9 (grown organically)

## WHAT'S IN MY PANTRY

- Extra-virgin olive oil for cooking and salad dressings
- Coconut Oil
- Red Palm Oil (for cooking & baking)
- Flavorful nut and seed oils for salad dressings and stir-fry seasonings: toasted sesame oil, walnut oil
- Vinegars: apple cider, organic red-wine vinegar, organic balsamic vinegar
- *Coconut Secret* Coconut Aminos (substitute for soy sauce, fish sauce)
- Kalamata olives, green olives
- Dijon mustard
- Ketchup
- Barbecue sauce
- Worcestershire sauce
- Sea Salt
- Black Pepper
- Dried organic herbs: bay leaves, dill, crumbled dried sage, dried thyme leaves, oregano, tarragon, Italian seasoning blend
- Spices: allspice (whole berries or ground), caraway seeds, chili powder, cinnamon sticks, ground cinnamon, coriander seeds, cumin seeds, ground cumin, curry powder, ground ginger, dry mustard, nutmeg, paprika, cayenne pepper, crushed red pepper, turmeric
- Raw Honey
- Coconut Sugar Stevia
- Pure maple syrup
- Unsweetened cocoa powder, natural and/or Dutch-processed
- Organic broths
- Organic Tomatoes & Tomato Paste in BPA-free cans (whole, crushed, diced, tomato paste/sauce)
- Wild caught Yellow Fin Tuna in BPA-free cans

- Pole caught/Wild caught Salmon
- Almond Flour (wheat alternative)
- Coconut Flour (wheat alternative)
- Buckwheat Flour (actually a seed, full of magnesium & packed w/protein)
- Chia/Hemp Seeds
- Flax Meal or Ground Flax Seed
- Organic Texmati White Rice
- Organic sprouted Quinoa
- Brown Rice (soaked overnight to reduce phytic acid in recipes)
- TruRoots Ancient Grains Pasta (gluten free)
- Walnuts (soak 4 hours, makes nuts more nutritious, dry by putting on cookie sheet in oven on low)
- Pecans (soak 8 hours)
- Almonds (soak overnight)
- Hazelnuts (soak overnight)
- Peanuts (soak overnight)
- Pine nuts (don't soak)
- Sesame seeds (overnight)
- Natural peanut butter
- Natural almond Butter
- Butter (organic from grass-fed cows)
- Reduced-fat mayonnaise
- Lemons, Limes & Oranges. The zest is as valuable as the juice. Organic fruit is recommended when using zest
- Onions
- Fresh garlic (in following recipes all cloves are size of index finger)
- Fresh ginger
- Fresh turmeric (I also store in freezer)

## WHAT IS IN MY FREEZER

- Meat: Lean, skinless chicken breast & thighs, extra-lean ground beef or turkey, fish fillets (salmon/tuna) or vegetarian alternatives
- Garden burgers or other veggie burgers
- Fat-free 100% turkey or beef franks, extra-lean turkey bacon, lean smoked turkey legs
- Vegetables with no salt added: spinach, broccoli, green beans, pre-made stir-fry mix, peas, corn, black-eyed peas, kale
- Unsweetened frozen fruit (berries, mango, cranberries, cut up slices of banana, fresh grated coconut)
- Waffles
- Naan bread

## WHAT IS IN MY FRIDGE

- Low-fat organic dairy products or dairy alternative: milk, yogurt, reduced-fat cheese/ almond milk/ Coconut milk
- Fresh Juices
- Eggs, egg substitute
- Lean deli meat: if packaged, select "natural" varieties with minimal processing/preservatives, and less than 20% of the daily value for sodium
- Natural jams
- Hummus
- Fresh fruit, unsweetened applesauce
- Fresh vegetables: salad greens, bagged chopped vegetables (broccoli, cauliflower), carrots, celery sticks, snap peas, tomatoes and mini tomatoes, green pepper, onion, greens (collard, kale) cabbage
- Whole wheat or other whole grain tortillas and pita pockets
- Condiments

# NOURISH a MAN, MARINATE a WOMAN

The first time I heard the statement "When we know better, we do better" by poet Maya Angelou, I thought, "Wow!" How simple, beautiful and freeing this statement is. This statement has allowed me to forgive myself for some bad decisions and be mindful of behaviors and people that were not good for me in my past. I realize looking back that I did not have the life skills, information, or maturity to handle certain situations that resulted in negative outcomes. Although I am responsible for my behaviors, this statement helped me let go of the guilt associated with them and has helped me vow to learn and do better.

We should take the same amount of time we do on watching other people and spend time watching ourselves. We pay attention as we walk into rooms and environments. We watch other people. We emulate other people. We wear their names. We wear their labels and their clothes. We try to follow their trends. We tune into their shows. We know everything about all the people we admire and nothing about ourselves. Maybe you need to date you so you can get to know yourself so deeply you value what you are giving away.

When you learn to take responsibility for yourself emotionally, physically, financially, spiritually, organizationally and relationally, then you will feel loved and lovable. Abandonment doesn't feel good. You wouldn't expect someone who loves you to abandon you, yet we do it to ourselves. Do you know the root of your challenge to find someone to be good to you? Start by looking at how you aren't being good to yourself.

Whether you are empty or full, it isn't about hunger for food, but the craving to reclaim and embrace your worth. Being full has nothing to do with stuffing your stomach or your schedule to capacity. There are many people who are busy, yet they are abandoning themselves instead of loving themselves. I have been very busy doing and not enough being. Expecting others to make you feel loved while you are abandoning yourself will never lead to feeling loved and lovable. Taking responsibility for loving yourself fills your heart with love, which you can then share with others.

Sharing love is the most fulfilling experience in life, but you need to be filled with love in order to have love to share. Understanding your worth and learning to love yourself is what fills you with love.

In 1966, the dynamic James Brown sang, "This is a man's world." Sadly, not much has changed. Only 17 of the world's 193 countries are led by women. The State of Women in America report revealed, women hold just 14 percent of executive officer positions and 18 percent of congressional seats. Factor in women of color, and the numbers are more disparaging, as they make up just 4 percent of top corporate jobs, 3 percent of board seats and 5 percent of congressional seats.

According to Sheryl Sandberg, Facebook COO and author of the self-described feminist platform *Lean In: Women, Work, and the Will to Lead*, this disparity in power and achievement can be attributed to systemic gender inequality and cultural biases, but also to something else: the way women are acculturated to respond, often subconsciously, to these factors. Sandberg calls on women to "lean in": to act with boldness and confidence; to "sit at the table" where decisions are made; to choose life partners who support their careers; and to not put those careers on hold for babies and marriage before you ascend the ladder.

Professional black women are bombarded with warnings about career and success. The bookshelves are filled with a genre of advice books instructing black women to, in effect, "lean back" (in my Fat Joe voice) in order to attract men. We are encouraged to think more about being chosen than choosing-making ourselves attractive to men by conforming to an "Act Like, Think Like" template of femininity.

By Sandberg's own admission; female executives are often viewed as being ultra-aggressive, cloak that with the spice of color, where assertive African American women are already labeled as 'the angry Black women' or 'bossy' and firm professional Latina women are tagged as being 'too opinionated' and brash. As an African-American woman living in a country that is far from post-gender, much less post- racial biases, I- and countless women like me- have had different experiences regarding issues such as ambition, finding the right mate, and family life balance.

I admit, it is difficult, as a woman, not to have the idea put into your head that no matter how objectively ordinary you may be, somehow you "deserve" to be with the cream of crop of male companionship. Read the covers of many women's magazines or scan the sound bites of most of the reality shows and you'll hear; "You deserve to be with a man who runs your bath every night. You deserve to be wined and dined, after a long day of shopping." Of course this dreamboat will have a six pack, and triceps that are always glistening, lips that are never ashy and eyes that are always easy to fall into.

Guys may have plenty of eye candy on the center spread of men's magazines, but read their advice columns (if there are any) and you won't read, "You deserve to have a woman that can play video games. You deserve a woman who will not just go to the golf course to ride on the cart- only to keep an eye on you. You deserve a woman who loves to watch football games with you. You deserve a woman who looks like a supermodel and will give you blow jobs every day!"

Maybe as ladies, we are confusing the term "deserve" with the term "desire". This is why even though many ladies feel there is nothing wrong with a blue collar worker, still renting, with kids, they still feel they deserve someone better.

I have found that you can always find taller, faster, slimmer, stronger or finer, but you'll never be satisfied with more until you're mindful with what you have now.

I overheard a high-school friend of mine talking with his fraternity brothers about breakups he had before he met his wife. Each of one of the guys had their own ideas about how women analyze men.

"I see it on social media," he said. Women will banter back and forth to their girlfriends, from head to toe about how a man measures up to their ideals. God forbid he is lacking something on their check list! They think about whether he can be fixed or upgraded to make him into what they want. Men, on the other hand, know that what you see is what you get. We either decide to deal with it or we don't."

Have you ever tried reading the ingredients on a box and imagining how something was going to taste? So why would you think you could ever get a clear picture of how someone is according to their social media sites? Posting a Bible scripture one day, a selfie at the club the next, talking about a client in a post next to the time line photo of their child's dance recital, sends mixed signals.

"Women talk about romantic love and a guy riding in to save the day, then, they turn around to analyze what he drove in on and how fast he was driving," Keith said. "They are hypocritical," he commented. "They say they want true love-but they have a long list of what it better come with. My wife isn't perfect, but I never feel like I settled. Women won't settle for a date, just to give a guy a chance. Well, men won't settle for what they want in a wife. We don't leave that to chance. We know what we want. If we haven't told you, you should have an idea it might not be you."

Do you know what you want? Do you want an intellectual or do you want someone who is curious and smart; a person with a Ph.D. may feel they know everything. What you need to look at isn't what you and someone have in common or the surface of what 'your type' is. You need to ask yourself, "Do we get each other?"

You want a strong man who cares about your feelings and has super powers to read your mind. You encourage him and you want to be President, but only as long as you have VETO power. Many of us will stay at a stable job, often boring and with an occasional fulfillment, rather than leaving it for our true passions, because it seems too risky.

"So you can compromise your choice of a job, but not your choice of a partner?" my Grandma V enquired. "You will spend eight hours or more a day in a good enough career instead of having enough faith in yourself to do what you love?"

I thought about this for a minute. "It's not the same," I said. "I have responsibilities. I can compromise in my career. I don't want to compromise about love."

My Grandma looked at me and laughed, "Girl, life and love are risky, but it's worth it. There are other fish in the sea, but how far in the deep end are you willing to go? The whole time you are swimming, there are other fish in the water with you. Don't confuse splashing for swimming," she continued. "Why are you going into it thinking you have to give up anything? You are already crossing things off your list before you even know what is on the paper."

What happens when you meet someone for the first time? Are you feeling them? Do you know what those feelings are? How do you feel when you hear from them, or when you don't?

How do you act? Are you waiting on them to call? Do you lose focus? Would your friends be able to recognize you? When your stomach is jumping, and you have butterflies flying around, you need to realize the feelings are a distraction from the things you feel that are important - your check list of standards.

Never settle for less than what you need and don't expect you can't get by without having everything on your checklist. Think about all the things people DON'T put on their check list. You may do better making a list of all the qualities each of your exes had, then review the list. In the end, what did any of those things mean to your decision?

You can't change another person. It's about deciding if you can accept things about the other person that you'd like to change, but can't.

# *SMOOTHIES*

**GREEN GOODNESS JUICE**

Great first thing in the morning or after a great workout

- 1medium RIPE pineapple
- 2 apples
- 1/2 lemon (peeled)
- 1/2 lime, washed including its peel
- 1bag of organic spinach
- 5 sticks celery
- 1whole cucumber, washed, including peel

JUICE, POUR, YUM!

***SMOOTHIE TIME SAVERS***

- Prepare frozen fruit ahead to save time and to prevent having to add ice, which waters your smoothie down. Cut and freeze on a baking sheet, then transfer to a freezer bag or container.

- Frozen bananas go a long way. Peel, slice, and freeze them. This go-to smoothie ingredient adds thickness without taking over other flavors. The below are selections great for all4 seasons of fruits.

- Add ingredients like coconut milk, yogurt, water, or juice first to get the blender moving. Then, add lighter, drier ingredients, like leafy greens, followed by heavy ingredients like fruit pieces.

## STRAWBERRY MANGO SMOOTHIE

Serves: 3 1/2 cups

- 1cup coconut milk
- 1banana, peeled, sliced, and frozen
- 1mango, skinned and chunked
- 5 large strawberries, stems cut off
- 1teaspoon peanut butter for *protein-optional*

Combine ingredients in blender and blend until smooth

## SUMMER SEASON SMOOTHIIE

Serves: 3 1/2 cups

- 1/2 cup Greek yogurt
- 1plum, pit removed, flesh roughly chopped
- 1peach, pit removed, flesh roughly chopped
- 1nectarine, pit removed, flesh roughly chopped
- 1/2 cup blueberries, fresh or frozen
- 1teaspoon chia/flax *seeds-optional*

Combine ingredients in blender and blend until smooth

## FALL FORWARD PUMPKIN SMOOTHIE

Serves: 3 1/2 cups

- 1cup almond milk
- 1teaspoon agave syrup
- 1cup pumpkin puree
- 2 teaspoons cinnamon
- 1apple, cored
- Dried cranberries for topping

Combine ingredients in blender and blend until smooth

## TUMMY TONIC GINGER BANANA SMOOTHIE

- 1 banana, sliced
- 3/4 cup (6 ounces) vanilla yogurt
- 3 kiwis frozen
- 1 tablespoon honey
- 1/2 teaspoon freshly grated ginger

Combine ingredients in blender and blend until smooth


## BEET IT SMOOTHIE

*High in magnesium, calcium, iron, potassium, and vitamins A and C. Don't worry, the beets add earthy sweetness with no strange aftertaste.*

- 2 apples, juiced (2/3 cup apple juice)
- 1 large beet juiced (about 3 tablespoons)
- 1 cup mixed berries
- 1 banana

Combine ingredients in blender and blend until smooth

Everyone tends to want to look their best when they are looking for a mate, but I challenge you to look good for yourself. Consuming the daily recommendations of fruits and vegetables can be a challenge. Blending a couple of servings of each into a smoothie helps ensure you meet your body's daily nutritional needs. I rotate the greens in my smoothies to avoid a buildup of alkaloids, compounds that can cause mild but unpleasant symptoms such as stomach aches. Here are a few reasons I enjoy smoothies:

- Smoothies are quick and easy. Making your own nutrient dense smoothie doesn't take as long as preparing most meals, giving you more time for others things. It's convenient to grab and go on my way out the door.
- I have to admit, when I am eating because I am emotional being healthy is the last thing on my mind. Fortunately, I love the taste of a creamy smoothie naturally sweetened by fruit or a good sweetener like honey, maple syrup, or stevia.
- You can provide your body with most of the vitamins and minerals it needs via smoothies. You should cut out the weight gaining snacks from your diet, drink plenty of water, and watch the pounds melt away. Lose weight easier than before and slim down the healthy way with smoothies.
- Smoothies are a natural 'relaxative'. Have you ever heard the term; 'full of sh!#?' Nobody I know wants to experience constipation or indigestion. Your blender can "chew" your food and ease the burden on your digestive system while you simultaneously consume plenty of dietary fiber to ensure excellent digestion.
- Detox. We're exposed to and bombarded by large amounts of man-made chemicals, which leaves our body begging to detoxify. Give your digestive system a break while adding detoxifying ingredients like dandelion greens and kale into your smoothies to aid your body's detoxification processes.
- Build muscle and improve work out performance. Provide your body with the nutrients and energy it needs to excel, recover and rebuild after working out. It's easier for your body to absorb and assimilate the nutrients in a smoothie as opposed to a meal.
- Beauty. Think radiant skin, hair, and nails. Supply your body with vitamins and minerals to grow healthier hair and make your skin glow.

*ADD INS:*

- *Hemp seeds* (Vegan protein source with a mild, nutty flavor)
- *Flax seed* (Rich in fiber, protein, and omega-3s)
- Wheat germ (One gram of dietary fiber per tablespoon)
- Sunflower seeds (Use shelled seeds for a boost of copper, magnesium, and selenium)
- Chia seeds (Fiber-loaded and protein-rich to control blood sugar; take on flavor of other ingredients)

 INDICATES VEGETARIAN

# GOIN' FISHIN'

My friends know I cook a lot, and sometimes they say it seems like I just toss in this or that and presto out comes something delicious! It seems like magic. So they often wonder how important it is to be accurate in measuring. The answer is: very important. Proper measuring is critical to cooking, even more so in baking. Baking is a science, and when you mix together ingredients, you're creating chemistry, albeit edible chemistry. So, being precise is important. There is balance between flour, *leaveners* (the things that make it rise), fats, and liquids.

Extra salt or baking soda can ruin otherwise great tasting cookies. Too much flour makes cakes taste dry and flavorless. When you start out cooking you shouldn't be nonchalant about measuring. The success of your recipe depends on it. Think about relationships. It takes that right measurements of bonding, what makes you rise, the right amount of stuff that will keep it all together makes up a successful relationship.

As you begin to feel more comfortable in the kitchen, you may experiment a bit. You may add some kisses to peanut butter cookies or throw some nuts into a batch of cookies. You may even substitute pecans for walnuts. The joys come in the variety, but give yourself time. You're never too good or experienced to measure in order to get things to your taste.

I invited my girlfriend over to show her how to make jerk chicken. I had been making it so long, I forgot the measurements. Measurements are guidelines, but they are useful when you're starting because it helps you figure out, each time, how you need to adjust to find the right combination. Because she has diabetes my salt and brown sugar quantities probably aren't good for her. So, we tried experimenting. During our time in the kitchen, she started telling me there were no good men in our city. I asked her if she wrote down her list of qualit*ies she wanted in a man*.

"You have to look at the measurements, the percentages of the ingredients," I said. "You just told me you were willing to compromise, but the more we talk about what you want in a man, the more rigid you get. You want to be with an African American man over six feet tall. Malcolm Gladwell, an English-Canadian journalist and bestselling author of *Tipping Point* and *Blink* states, only 14% of the United States population of men are above 6' 1 and 80% of the available women want to have them. Most of that 80% are not going to compromise. Do the math. Divide that by the percentage that are African American and then factor in that 90% of the available African American women want them, plus 30% from every other race. Figure it out! How can no less than 70 % of women get 15 % of men?"

I want you to stop reading for a moment and do it yourself. Write down the characteristics you are looking for, then calculate the percentage of men available who meet those criteria (You can do a search on the internet). It wasn't a precise science, but my girlfriend and I did this together. We estimated the percentages of men who are smart enough, funny enough, faith-filled enough, successful enough, family-oriented enough, kid-friendly enough, unselfish enough, kind enough, attractive enough, are currently single, emotionally available, like the opposite sex, in my age group and live in the general area of Columbus, Ohio. Our conclusion was only about four percent of the local male population.

Then we did a deeper calculation. Even if the four percent met our requirements, what were the chances that we would meet theirs? How many of those men were looking for what we had to offer? How many of those four percent were looking for a nearly forty year old? Now the dating pool gets smaller. What if my requirement to be 'faith filled' meant the same religion, because I have learned it is important to me that we worship together? My final calculation would look more like 2 %.

If you want to be even more specific in your criteria, be prepared for the numbers to dwindle down further. Things like, I'm an urban gardener who enjoys neo-soul, and the man I'm with has to feel the same way about respecting the environment as I do.

"Are you for real right now?" my girlfriend Yvonne asked. "Frankly, if someone wants to put up with your O.C.D, you need to allow them the opportunity."

I wouldn't have ever classified myself or my girlfriends as picky, just selective. However, I have learned, in talking to friends like Nicci Carr Sprouse, CEO of Columbus Ohio's *Dating League*, that you have to start with knowing what you want. In addition, you may have to consider working with a professional to understand the skill in knowing just enough about someone, so the fantasy about that person can build.

It's one thing for a partner to accept your interests It's another thing entirely to ask them to feel the way you do about them. Moreover, with all of the requirements you expect the person to have, you are lowering the percentage of opportunity to find a match. Do you really know what you want? Our desires change through time as we deal with life circumstances, such as financial issues, career goals and changes and children.

When you are first dating, you are on your best behavior. Bad habits are hidden. You usually try to look your best, act your best, talk your best, and be your best at all times! You are attentive. You go out of your way to do small things for each other. When you are first dating, your manners are front of mind. You wouldn't dream of belching or farting in front of each other. That would be horribly embarrassing! You think twice before answering your cell or sending texts at the dinner table. That's rude! You are mindful about the others time

As your relationship progresses, however, you start to become more comfortable with each other, and that, can be a simultaneously very good thing, and a very bad thing. I enjoy the time after the formality disappears and the comfort level around each other increases. It transitions relationships to a new level. But, can relationships become too comfortable? Should relationships hang on to some of that formality, that level of trying to "impress" each other, that ability to always be on your best behavior, in order to be most successful?

On a sweltering hot summer day you can get into an air conditioned car and think it is the best thing you have ever felt, only to turn on your radio and forget the cool air 30 minutes later. You get used to it, and it's not so wonderful anymore, or at least your enthusiasm for it has changed-it's expected.

My son has wanted to be a lawyer since he was eight years old. Harvard gets about 35,000 applications each year. Harvard doesn't feel insulted when someone with a low GPA or SAT score applies. They simply send a non-selection letter. They don't get mad or feel insulted at who applies, even if they aren't qualified. However, the difference between you and Harvard is Harvard accepts nearly 9% of their applicants each year and you don't. Maybe you don't have Ivy League standards, but you still want a good candidate. The Ohio State University has slightly over 42,000 applicants each year and 7,000 incoming freshman. This is still a better percentile than you are willing to give possible suitors.

Let more people into your circle that could make you happy, or you can hold out for the small percentage of men you *assume* meet your requirement and hope by some chance that someone in that 3% feels that you are in his 3%. Reflect on the guys who are now your exes. At one time you thought they were for you. The ones you gave a chance were based on what you thought you were looking for and, in fact, didn't end up being what you wanted.

It's not that there aren't any good men out there. It's just according to your criteria you can't recognize them. The world is full of good men, who have lists of their own. When starting out dating, you may have to stretch what you are measuring. You catch more fish with a net than with a hook.

"But, what if you feel the bait you have on your hook is there to attract a specific catch?" Dorian asked. "You don't want to just date anyone."

"How many fish have pulled on your line?" I asked. "Not how many have swam by opening their gills, but how many have actually been nibbling at the hook? Maybe the net you're fishing with looks more like a hair net."

I could hear crickets. The point isn't that there's only one fish in five thousand out there for you. It's that you may be overlooking fish that might push your percentages up higher. You need to use a better net, until you understand how to qualify what is a good match.

When there are things you may find unappealing about a person, try to be more accepting than judgmental. If a guy has typos in his email to you, don't assume he's illiterate. Take into consideration that he was nervous, or that he may have had several things going on at his office that day. Think of reasons why he could be a winner before you assume he is a loser. Ask yourself this question. If an interesting guy was standing in front of you, would you honestly count them out because their brown shoes don't go with his black pants or because he has a couple more inches around his waist than you envisioned? If you would, that's cool, but don't complain that you can't find a man because you disqualified him on a technicality. The truth of it is, if everyone looked close enough, we could all find technicalities. This would mean you would have to accept being disqualified too. Don't get so focused on whether you're interested in someone that you forget whether they would be interested in you.

I attempted to sit down and write a list of what I wanted in a man when I was in my early twenties. It later turned into a list of what I didn't want in my early forties. I have a girlfriend who is being weighed down by the biological clock in her head and it's impairing her list. She claims she doesn't have one, but I think she does, even if it only exists in her head.

"I can't articulate what I'm looking for," she says. "I always end up hooking up, hoping to fall in love."

Then, after she sat down at my table with a glass of wine, it took her less than five minutes to give me a detailed description of the qualities she felt her dream guy would possess. There were over thirty-three items on her list. So I suggested she narrow her list to make it a bit more realistic.

"I don't want to settle!" She protested.

"I'm not asking you to settle. I have a man and I don't feel like I settled. I finally understood what was important in order to stand the test of time and it wasn't a list of over thirty characteristics."

She gave it a try and crossed out a few surface items; he doesn't have to be 6 foot 2 inches, over 5 feet 8 would be fine, he doesn't have to like to shop, she could find a mall with a restaurant that has a bar and a TV where he could hang out and she could be cool with that. She saw it wasn't about what he had, but what he gave.

I went down to the basement to dig out the last list I wrote. There were a few qualifications that had been crossed out, but I had circled them and placed an asterisk next to each of them:

*How many sweet gestures done?* How often does he have to perform these gestures before you can qualify someone as romantic? How many times in a day or in a week can you be touched or caressed to label someone as passionate? What is the line between a person who has a sense of humor and someone who belongs on stage at the Funny Bone?

My own list exposed a dilemma of variables. I would never say the man described on my girlfriend's paper didn't exist. All of us have lists for prospective suitors. What I am suggesting is that some of the qualities on our lists aren't standards that we hold ourselves to, but expectations that we are projecting onto others.

Scratch off anything on your list as a deal breaker which may be objective (height, age, what type of job he has, how muscular he is, whether he has kids, a baby's momma, or an ex-wife) and start to examine what's subjective (maturity, sense of humor, ability to commit, generosity and sensitivity). I am the first to say that when I was single and in my twenties, I wanted it all: athletic, entrepreneurial, handsome, intelligent, funny, nice faded haircut, Armani suited. I was very specific. While I got most (but not all) of what I wanted, I am quick to point out that none of that has to do with happiness in marriage. The most important qualities that are critical in my marriage were selflessness, humility, faith, and communication style. I can't express how many times a day you have to decide whether to maximize your happiness or the other person's. It's shouldn't be seen as only a female expectation, nor is it emasculating for in a man. It's about caring. So, I ask you to consider, how you rank selflessness, faith and humility when you are rejecting a guy based on his age and the model of car he's driving?

"If you don't chose anything-you are left with nothing" ~ Anonymous

# *THE DISH on FISH*

**SWIMMINGLY TASTY FISH STICKS**
* Choose wild over farmed fish.
Serves:4

- 1pound wild white fish (can be frozen & thawed)
- 2 large eggs, whisked
- 1cup of organic almond flour
- 1teaspoon of unrefined sea salt
- lemon squeezed
- Coconut oil for frying

Clean and pat dry fish and cut into strips. (remove bones as you cut) Whisk eggs in a small bowl and place the almond flour mixed with salt on a plate.

Heat Oil. Coat each fish strip with egg mixture and dip both sides in almond flour. Place on a clean plate until the oil is hot (check heat by adding a pinch of flour to see if it bubbles).

Fry both sides of the strips until brown and crispy. Serve with organic vinegar or favorite condiments.

## CATCH A FISH COUSCOUS:
Serves 4

- 2 tablespoons olive oil
- 2 red onions; sliced into thin rings
- 2 tablespoons raisins
- 3 tablespoons salted roasted cashew nuts
- 1 red bell pepper; seeded and sliced into thick rings
- 1 yellow bell pepper; seeded and sliced into thick rings
- 1 green bell pepper; seeded and sliced into thick rings
- 4 fresh firm ripe Roma tomatoes; blanched and sliced into thick rounds
- 1 ½ cups fish or vegetable stock or ¾ cup fortified wine (such as sweet sherry or Madeira) mixed with ¾ cup water
- 1 ½ pounds (750 g) red snapper or swordfish fillets cut into 1 ¼ inch cubes
- Sea salt, freshly ground black pepper
- 1 tablespoon chopped fresh parsley

*Couscous*:

- 2 cups quick-cooking couscous
- 2 cups vegetable stock or water; boiling,
- 2 or 3 teaspoons grass-fed butter or unrefined organic coconut oil
- ½ teaspoon Sea salt (optional)
- 

Heat half the oil in a large heavy-based skillet and sauté half the onions on medium to high heat for 6 to 8 minutes, or until very dark golden, stirring all the time. Using a slotted spoon, remove the fried onions from the oil, place them on paper towels, and set aside. Fry the raisins in the same hot oil until they plump. Remove with the slotted spoon and add to the friend onions. Fry the cashews for about 1 minute. Remove and add to the raisin-and-onion mix.

Add the remaining oil to the skillet and fry the other half of the onions until golden. Add the bell peppers and continue cooking for about 10 minutes or until the peppers are soft. Add the tomatoes and the stock, partially cover, and cook for about 10 minutes on medium to low heat.

Stir the fish through the onion and pepper mixture. Taste and season with salt and pepper. Continue simmering for 10 minutes or until the fish is tender. Do not forget to stir periodically to prevent sticking. To make the couscous, place the couscous grains in a large, deep dish with a lid. Pour in the boiling stock and stir in the butter and salt. Cover and set aside to keep warm for about 15 minutes so the couscous can absorb the liquid and swell up.

Carefully pour the fish mixture over the couscous and gently fold it through to mix thoroughly into a colorful presentation. Sprinkle with the onion rings, raisins, cashew nuts and the parsley. Serve hot immediately.

**LEMONY-GINGER FISH:**
Serves 4 to 6:

- 1 ½ pounds (750 g) whole fish (such as wild snapper cleaned and scaled)
- 1 tablespoon peeled and very finely grated   fresh ginger
- 2 tablespoons lemon thyme
- 1 tablespoon olive oil
- sea salt, freshly ground black pepper
- ¼ red bell pepper; seeded and sliced into thin strips,
- ¼ yellow bell pepper; seeded and sliced into thin strips
- ¼ green bell pepper; seeded and sliced into thin strips
- 1 small red onion; sliced into thin strips
- 1 tablespoon cornstarch blended with 2 tablespoons cold water
- Cilantro springs; for garnish
- flat-leaf parsley sprigs; for garnish.

*Sauce:*

- 2 tablespoons olive oil
- 3 green onions; minced
- 2 cloves garlic; minced
- 1 tablespoon peeled and finely grated fresh ginger
- 3 organic Portobello mushrooms; clean and sliced into very thin strips
- 1 ½ tablespoons organic cane sugar
- 1 tablespoon ground turmeric
- 2 tablespoons tamarind paste blended with 1 tablespoon hot water

- 2 cups vegetable stock
- 1 tablespoon fish sauce
- salt, freshly ground black pepper.

Preheat the oven to 350 F/180 C

Have your grocer scale and clean the fish, as well as trim off the fins and tail.

Place the fish on a chopping board, and dry with a paper towel. Using a sharp knife, carefully make 2 deep, diagonal cuts (about ¾ inch apart) across the full length of the fish in the fleshy part. Repeat the same cuts traveling in the opposite direction to form a crisscross pattern on the fish. Do not cut down on the bone. Turn the fish over and repeat the same pattern of cuts.

Mix together the ginger, lemon thyme, and olive oil and season with salt and pepper. Stuff the seasoning into the cuts on both sides, making sure that every cut is well filled with the seasoning. Rub any remaining seasoning on the body of the fish and into the head.

Grease a sheet of foil. Loosely wrap the seasoned fish and bake for about 20 to 30 minutes, or until the fish flakes when tested with a fork. While the fish is baking, prepare the sauce.

To make the sauce, heat the oil in a large skillet and sauté the green onions, garlic ginger, and mushrooms over low to medium heat for about 5 minutes. Add the sugar and continue to cook for 3 minutes.

Stir in the turmeric, tamarind paste, vegetable stock, and fish sauce. Taste and season with salt and pepper. Continue cooking on low heat for 5 minutes. Add the red, yellow, and green bell peppers and the onion, and cook for approximately 3 minutes. Mix in the cornstarch and stir until the sauce thickens.

Pour the juices from the baked fish into the pan and stir to mix. Arrange the baked fish on a large plate, and spoon the sauce over it. Garnish with the parsley and cilantro. Serve immediately.

**FISH TACOS**

*Tacos:*

- 1pound white flaky fish, mahi mahi
- 1/4 cup olive/coconut oil
- 1lime, juiced
- 1tablespoons chipotle/ chili powder
- 1jalapeno, coarsely chopped
- 1/4 cup chopped fresh cilantro leaves
- 8 flour/corn tortillas

*Garnish:*

- Shredded white cabbage/romaine lettuce
- Hot sauce
- Sour cream
- Thinly sliced red onion
- Thinly sliced green onion
- Chopped cilantro leaves
- Pureed Tomato salsa

Preheat grill to medium-high heat. Place fish in a medium size bowl. Whisk together the oil, lime juice, chipotle powder, jalapeno, and cilantro and pour over the fish. Let marinate for 15 to 20 minutes. Remove the fish from the marinade, place onto a hot skillet, flesh side down. Grill the fish for 4 minutes on the first side and then flip for 30 seconds and remove. Let rest for 5 minutes then flake the fish with a fork.

Place the tortillas on the skillet and grill for 20 seconds. Divide the fish among the tortillas and garnish with any or all of the garnishes.

## HONEY LOVE & GINGER GLAZED SALMON
Serves: 6

- 1/2 cup orange juice
- 1/4 cup soy sauce
- 2 Tbsp. fresh ginger, finely chopped
- 1 small jalapeno chopped
- 2 Tbsp. honey
- 1 tsp. toasted sesame oil
- 1 fillet of salmon (2 pounds; preferably wild), skin on, cut into 6 equal pieces
- 2 Tbsp. extra-virgin olive oil

In a small saucepan, bring orange juice, soy sauce, ginger, jalapeno, honey, and sesame oil to a simmer over high heat. Reduce to medium-low; cook 5 minutes. Pour half of marinade into a shallow dish large enough to hold fish in a single layer; cool 10 minutes. Add fish; coat with marinade. Turn skin side up. Cover with plastic; set aside 10 minutes.

In large frying pan, heat olive oil over medium-high heat. Place fish in pan skin side down; cover and cook until skin is crisp, about 3 minutes. Flip and cook 2 to 3 minutes more.

## WISHY FISHY GRITS  (*to substitute fish for tempch, see below)

- 3/4 cup chicken or vegetable broth
- 1/2 teaspoon sea salt
- 2 tablespoons minced red onion
- 1 garlic clove, minced
- 1 1/2 cups water
- 1/2 cup regular grits
- 1 teaspoon olive oil
- 2 tablespoons grated Parmigiano-Reggiano or fresh Parmesan cheese
- 4 (6-ounce) wild salmon fillets (about 1 inch thick) w/skin -(*1/2 pound tempeh)
- 1/4 teaspoon sea salt

- 1/4 teaspoon dried thyme
- 1 teaspoon cayenne
- 1/4 teaspoon black pepper
- Cooking spray
- 2 teaspoons finely chopped fresh parsley

Combine first 4 ingredients in a small saucepan. Bring to a boil; reduce heat, and simmer 5 minutes or until onion is tender. Add water; bring to a boil. Gradually add grits, stirring with a fork until smoothly blended. Cover, reduce heat, and simmer 10 minutes or until done.

Preheat broiler.

Heat the oil in a small nonstick skillet over medium-high heat. Stir grated cheese into grits. Set aside. Sprinkle fillets with sea salt, thyme, cayenne, and pepper; place the fillets, skin sides down, on a broiler pan coated with olive or coconut oil cooking spray. Broil for 10 minutes or until fish is pink & flakes easily when tested with a fork. Remove skin from fillets; discard skin. Spoon 1/2 cup grits on each plate; top each serving with salmon. Sprinkle with parsley.

*Cut the tempeh into 1/2 inch pieces. Cut those pieces in 1/2 widthwise.

In a medium-size saucepan, combine 3 cups of vegetable stock and 1/2 teaspoon sea salt. Stir until the salt dissolves, then add the tempeh. Bring to a boil, lower the heat to medium high, cover and simmer for 20 minutes, until the tempeh is moist and drowned in vegetable broth. Remove from heat, drain the tempeh in a colander (save stock), and let the pieces dry for 30 minutes.

Using a paper bag; combine (1 teaspoon each) thyme, cayenne, onion powder, pepper, oregano and 1 teaspoon of sea salt. Shake until coated.

In a large skillet over medium-high heat, warm the olive/coconut oil. Add the tempeh and saute for 3 minutes, until golden brown-turn and continue cooking on the other side until golden brown. Quickly place drained tempeh back into paper bag and shake until coated on all sides.

## GRILLED STUFFED RED SNAPPER
Serves: 6

- 3 tablespoons butter
- 3/4 cup fresh bread crumbs
- 1/4 cup chopped scallions (green onions)
- 1/3 cup celery, diced (1 large celery stalk)
- 1 clove garlic, minced
- 1 teaspoon dried thyme
- 4 ounces cooked shrimp (optional) can use diced carrots
- 4 ounces cooked crabmeat (optional)
- 2 tablespoon chopped fresh baby spinach
- 1 tablespoon fresh chopped parsley
- 1/8 teaspoon sea salt
- 1/8 teaspoon ground black pepper
- 6 (4 ounce) fillets red snapper (I sometimes use 3 whole snappers- scaled, no head, cleaned & butterfly)

Preheat coals in a covered grill to high heat (if you aren't grilling, you can bake in oven at 350 F for 18 minutes). Rub fish w/ lemon or lime juice, set aside.

*To Make Stuffing:* Melt 2 tablespoons butter or margarine in a skillet. Add the bread crumbs. Saute and stir the mixture over medium-high heat till the bread crumbs are browned. Remove the bread crumbs to a mixing bowl.

Melt 1 tablespoon butter or margarine in the skillet and saute the onions, celery, carrots (if not adding shrimp/crab) and garlic until tender; add to bread crumbs in mixing bowl, then stir in shrimp, crab, parsley, spinach, thyme salt and pepper and toss gently.

Cut foil to form a double-thickness 18x12-inch rectangle. Lay the fish fillets on the double thickness of foil. Mound the stuffing on top of the fillets.

Curl up the edges of the foil to form a tray. In a covered grill, arrange the preheated coals at either side of the grill. Test for medium heat above the center of the grill. Place the fish in foil in the center of the grill rack. Cover and grill for 20 to 25 minutes or just until the fish flakes easily.

*To cook whole fish*

Why slap a whole fish on the grill? Because it tastes better: The skin protects the delicate flesh, the bones keep it juicy, and you can stuff the cavity with flavorful citrus (for a sweeter taste- use clementines, for tangy-use lemons no peel) and herbs. Important, clean the grill and brush it with oil right before cooking.

*Score It:* fish are scored deeply before grilling. The cuts help distribute heat so the fish cooks evenly.

Slice at an angle all the way to the bone, repeating every 11/2". Use an extra-sharp knife-you want clean cuts, not mangled flesh.

*Stuff It:* Sprinkle fish with salt and pepper on each side, plus another pinch of each in the cavity. Place vegetable, herb and citrus stuffing inside.

*Oil It:* Coat fish with about 1Tbsp. olive oil. Or place on oiled foil & wrap for easy turning

# WHEN TO SAY WHEN: LEFT OVERS & DO-OVERS

"Clean up as you go. Drink while you cook. Make it fun. It doesn't have to be complicated."

I had my share of disappointments before I was old enough to date. My parents signed me over to be adopted. I grew up as the literal black sheep and minority in my family; I was never delusional to feel that I was perfect. I knew that if I was ever to get married, he would be a flawed human being like me. I wasn't expecting perfection, but I did want an intense connection. I'm not talking about the light headed-sitting by the phone- expecting him to call excitement. I'm talking about the feeling that when something important happens, he is the first one I want to call. These feelings let me know that there was enough feeling to get us off the ground.

Maybe there isn't a secret recipe to finding the perfect match, but there are some key ingredients. First, find out if you and the guy have common relationship goals. Second, look at the values the two of you share- family life, children, religion, loyalty, individuality. Third, find out what are the key qualities you need? Lastly, (just as when you are making meringue,-success depends on following the order.) find out your shared interests. Interests are usually the first thing people share with each other, because people think it's bonding (many of these interests could be found on a Facebook page), but the first three ingredients are more important for a long term relationship.

I look back and see areas where I thought having someone with the same drive in their career, same community commitment or dedication to the gym was important. I have learned that two intelligent people, with a sense of humor, coming from similar backgrounds and valuing similar things, will often get together and find they have some similar interests.

Think about it. If you both like the idea of raising a family together, and want to be married, then the cigar smoking and golf outings aren't much of an issue. People often think they have to choose between a few narrow qualities such as looks, intelligence and title, but you'd probably be happy with someone who has an acceptable degree of each. No one would expect you to choose between a guy who is a two on looks, an eight on intelligence and unemployed and another guy who is an eight on looks, and a two in intelligence. Eliminate title, because if he isn't very smart, he won't have much of a title. Most often, you'll be faced with a guy who might be a six on looks, seven on intelligence and eight on personality. What you'll find is a pretty rounded individual.

There's a group of ladies who may consider this settling, because you want someone who is an eight in every area. However, others would consider this a good deal. That same group of ladies will look at those who they considered as settling with their husbands, families and commitment and say, "I wonder what it would be like to have what she has?" It could have been theirs to have, but they passed it up.

There's a difference between what would make a good boyfriend and who would make a good husband. You shouldn't base your decision on the big gestures, but the small acts of kindness like making you tea if you're congested and filling up your car with gas. When dating, we mistake romance for selflessness, but you find it's not the same thing. That's why I smile when I see friends posting pictures of the flowers they received at the office. Romantic gestures like sending flowers aren't the same thing as checking to see if your car has gas before your work week begins or waking up in the middle of the night and taking care of a sick child so you can sleep.

I get quite a few of my girlfriends who will say they aren't going to settle. I don't think you should settle. You should look at it as broadening your fantasies. We've all been hurt and felt the need to be guarded. Don't mistake a white picket fence for a brick wall. When you are closed off, you limit what you can receive.

Why are people so worried about settling, when we find ourselves unhappily unsettled and sleeping in a one half warm, other half cold bed, eating takeout dinner- while watching reality shows in front of the TV- because we think grocery shopping or having a refrigerator that's full of food when there is only one person in the house is a waste of time, while dreaming of a guy who will reveal himself so we can settle-down.

One of the biggest misconceptions single women make is that consistency equals boring and that compromise is a bad word. Sometimes the reason you may not think you have found Mr. Right is because you are wrong about the qualities Mr. Right should possess. Unfortunately, some of us don't realize the most important qualities in a 'keeper' until we have had to throw a few back.

Lose the fear of losing him. If he is meant for you he will be for you. Love and fear are two strong emotions, and it is difficult for the both of them to occupy the same space. If you want to accept love, you have to open up and release your fear. One of the best ways to beat fear is with knowledge. If you are going into the relationship giving what you'd expect to get, you should be confident, that's what you're going to get back. Pay attention to the compliments he gives you, more than likely those are the things that have his attention. So, those are the strengths to which you need to pay attention. If you feel so fondly about him, know that the qualities you have, that attracted him, deserves some celebrating too.

Ladies shouldn't expect anyone else to build your Self-confidence. Being in a relationship is often referred to as a 'plus one' when responding to an invitation. This reference would imply you are already one. You are number one, and anyone else is an addition.

You shouldn't be swayed to stay with someone because you feel the percentage of good men is low. A good man would want to claim a good woman. Don't stay in a relationship hoping you found a good one, because if you are wondering, it should serve as a warning sign. Letting go can mean the timing is bad. However, you shouldn't be tied to, or give your attention and your confidence to someone when there is someone else waiting for you to free up an opportunity to show you they are really the best choice for you.

Here are a few common examples that can cue the need for a detour:

- You shouldn't say you don't mind if your mate goes to girls/guys night or whatever when actually you do mind.

- Responding with "Nothing's wrong" or "I'm fine", when there's something wrong and you're absolutely *not* fine, will not get you to a solution quickly.

- Saying; "So, this guy/girl at work told me I'm cute today. I think he/she *don't believe* how many guys/girls made comments on your page. Why do you feel the need to mention that? Are you saying those people are somebody about whom your date should be concerned? Are they a threat? What purpose does this serve? Pushing buttons and manipulating feelings is reckless. It's like texting and driving. You may get your message across, but you'll be the one getting hurt in the process.

- (Strictly for the fellas) Unsolicited shots of your penis are not something beside it that would give some size perspective; like a can of Red Bull or a roll of life savers. (just kidding)

- Taking selfies with someone who is just getting to know you, could lead someone is trying to be nice or polite by having a conversation, it shouldn't be considered desperate or thirsty and at risk for a grand, public ostracizing on social media.

- If a man prefers to text you than call you, he is not that into you. A why he is your best choice. Texting is not communicating.

Will Smith's character in, *Hitch*, a romantic comedy said, "Sixty percent of all human communication is nonverbal, body language. Thirty percent is your tone".

So that means that ninety percent of what you're saying isn't coming out of your mouth. If 90% of what you're communicating doesn't come from your mouth, don't expect correct interpretation from your fingers. Texting may be convenient, but showing the extra effort lets someone know they matter to you.

Navigating through the ups and downs of a relationship can be challenging. It's not about balancing a steady 50/50 in the middle. Healthy relationships are about two people who are willing to make adjustments for each other, in real time and as needed. Two people must be willing to give more when the other person can't help but give a little less.

It's not about finding someone in which to *lose* yourself. It's about meeting someone in whom you *find* yourself. Neither of you start off meeting the best in each other. You will both grow into your best selves by spending time together and nurturing each other's growth.

As you think about what you and some of your closest confidants add to each other's lives, you will often find that instead of giving and taking things from each other (advice, answers, gifts), you have chosen rather to share in other's joys and pain while experiencing life together.

Keep in mind we can't manipulate anyone to be with us or love us. We shouldn't beg someone to stay when they want to leave. Likewise, we should never feel trapped in a relationship. Being trapped will make you feel that you are doing less to navigate and more to survive the relationship. Relationships are about freedom and the strength of a relationship depends on the strength of the two people in it.

When you meet a person, keep in mind that everyone has a story. Everyone has gone through something that has changed them and forced them to grow. Every face represents a story every bit as compelling and complicated as yours. It's important to remember that some people you meet may be going through a difficult stage in their lives, and although there is always time to be kind, there's never time to be blind. Never give time to someone who wants to play with your feelings just because they are unsure of their own.

When life gives you lemons make lemonade, but what's the recipe? Just add a spoonful of optimistic sugar? It sounds good, but the ideal recipe calls for a little background.

When we subscribe to a cell phone carrier we make a deliberate choice. Subscribing to a belief is more often an impulsive decision, an unconscious commitment to ideas and values that affirm us in our practical commitments to what we do, whom we love, or how we live.

Our beliefs grow like roots, stabilizing and nurturing our sense of being successful in our everyday lives. The longer we've been planted in one place, the more our beliefs will tend to accumulate and reinforce our residence there. Beliefs affirm who, what, how and where we are. Beliefs that rationalize why we're doing what we're doing and not doing all those other things we could do. We think that it's *I'll do it when I believe in it*, but more often than not it's *I'll believe in it when I'm doing it*.

Call it a measure of personal success, not just to yourself, but to the company you keep, the career you've landed and the decisions you've made. These beliefs justify your right to say, "Yes, I intended this. I belong here. This is the right place to be."

We're much more inclined to subscribe to beliefs that credit our position in life than ones that discredit. Keeping alignment with our beliefs is always easier to swallow than the sour taste of weakness through indecisiveness.

You shouldn't stay in a relationship for years because you have aligned with beliefs that affirm why being *coupled* is better and being single is worse. If you have a break-up you have to re-root yourself, swapping out your former beliefs for new beliefs that affirm why living life *un-coupled* is better and being *coupled-up* is worse. You will start to question your beliefs. Losing what we valued to re-root into what we devalued is enough to make any of us insecure and can taste as sour as lemons.

Our personal beliefs play a huge role in how we view our own life. Your estimation of your successes and failures will depend entirely on the framework of your personal beliefs. Our beliefs provide a structure to help us feel safe and secure.

We all have an inherent and insatiable desire to feel safe and secure. Efforts to fill this desire shape our actions. This is why we are subconsciously programmed to make reality fit our core beliefs about who we are and what we deserve. When our perception of the world validates our beliefs, we feel secure in the fact that our view is the correct one.

We will attract, and be attracted to, people who confirm our beliefs. This is why some people experience one bad relationship after another. They continue to be attracted to people who affirm their limiting beliefs about themselves.

Something deep inside them believes that they don't deserve to have a happy, meaningful relationship. This same 'something' is irresistibly attracted to, and attracts, the very person who will validate their perceived worthlessness.

So how does one make lemonade when re-rooting? How does one swap out the old beliefs and values for new ones? You recall past experiences about how you gradually swapped out your former beliefs and values for new ones and how it turned out to be well worth it. You gain confidence when you look back on how you weren't broken, how you grew, and what you gained from your re-rooted circumstances.

There isn't just one possible future. So there is no single recipe for getting from the sourness of the present to some future sweetness. We are all guessing on how to make the best of our circumstances, keeping open minds rather than subscribing exclusively to one official future. Courting prior to commitment keeps you tuned in and opens to opportunities as they arise.

In the crisis of re-rooting, people tend to panic and shrink their tolerance for more expansive thought about how the world works and how to work within the world. If our internal recipe of relationships is built on limiting beliefs, life becomes a great big negative reinforcement loop. So, the question remains, how do we create a new recipe that serves us?

Did you ever notice when you receive a complement on an improvement, you are torn at acceptance at the risk insulting your former self? For example, someone saying you look like you lost weight implies that you were fat before?

The same effect applies when you imagine complementing yourself on your own future growth. To imagine having become a better person means admitting that now you're not all you can be, not a welcome thought in the midst of starting to date, since it tends to make us defensively self-protective.

See, our most valuable ingredients aren't the ones that hold us to our present situations but to our present selves, especially in the indignity of being exiled to new soil. The last thing we think we can afford to let go of is our sense that we were right all along. It's humiliating to admit we were wrong. Our stomach pangs for a lost partner or lost situation, is more often an ache for lost confidence in ourselves. That discomfort is the sour that lingers longest.

If you redefine yourself as a work in progress, if you sketch out how that work might go, if you can swap out your former self-worth for the prospect of earning still more dignity by learning, it may be just the sip you need to taste the sweetness and speak life to yourself. It is an opportunity to have a life grounded in optimism about the process of slowly, but surely, moving forward.

The bottom line is this: when you change your beliefs, you change your recipe. Building your internal empowering beliefs will transform the way you experience your life.

Of course, the smart cook reads every recipe all the way through before proceeding, but sometimes we're in a hurry. And even then, no recipe should bury difficult or time-consuming steps or make the cook have to do a special on line order just to retrieve the ingredients needed for the dish.

I tried to pick recipes that while being regionally sensitive to what ingredients are available. (That's why I didn't include some of my favorite African dishes) I also was cognoscente to the level of tolerance of my sons, who helped me at all hours either as Guiney pigs or record keepers while compiling the recipes. I am proud that irritation did not cause them to emancipate themselves from me and change their names. I had my own recipe pet peeves while learning to cook. The flaws on how they are written can be adjusted with practice, but flaws on substance can ruin your confidence in the kitchen.

We all have flaws. We have shared how you can misjudge someone based on first appearance or first encounter. You first introduction to lemons may have been un-friendly. Now that you are grown and have experienced many flavors you know it can sweeten anything from cake to cocktails. People don't come with instructions. They can sweeten your life or they can turn it sour and put us in life-puckering situations that ruin our confidence in relationships.

The emotionally unstable have a need to be at the center of your attention and their needs always come first. Having a bad day? Well, that's too bad. They don't hear you. They need you to stop what you are doing and attend to them. Want to argue logic to emotion with them? Don't. You won't win with them. Emotions and arguing trump rationality and logic. Want to explain what really happened or your intentions? Don't bother. They aren't vested in your feelings, the truth or your side of the argument. This relationship will either have you constantly on guard or constantly pulling out your pom poms.

You are either for them or against them. There is no in between. They can be exciting, both sexually and socially, but always demanding and that is where they wear you out. They dread being abandoned (They will remind you of all the others that did.) and will do anything to keep you around. These people are blind to their own toxic actions that often drive those that care for them away.

In a relationship like this, you end up feeling exhausted because you are tethered toxically to a person who controls you through their emotions. You feel as though you have to be careful what you do and say even though they have the freedom to do and say (or flirt) as they wish. You have to tip toe, sacrifice, and be mindful and attentive.

It doesn't matter how you got into the relationship. What's important is the realization that it is one sided, exploitive and toxic. Ask yourself a few questions: Do you find yourself 'bracing' yourself before you take their call? Do you feel manipulated? Do you feel like this relationship is one sided? Are you hurting in this relationship?" If the answer to these questions is yes, it is time to cut them loose and get your life back.

If a man tells you that the previous women he has dealt with are crazy, trust the red flag. Either he is the one who is crazy or he has done something consistently to take them out of their element. When you feel like it's a red flag, don't keep asking yourself if it is a red flag. It's a red damn flag!

The sad truth is that there are some people who will only be there for you as long as you have something they need. When you no longer serve a purpose to them, they will leave. The other truth is that the crazy ones never want to lose you. The good news is, if you tough it out, you will get better at recognizing them earlier, it won't take you as long to weed them out and you will be left with a real winner. Fishing is part skill and part patience, but it is also a sport and all sports started out as games.

There's a game commonly being played in the dating world called, 'I'm Going to Prove That You're Into This WAY More Than I Am'. It's as if someone told you they would reward you for being a Debbie or Donald Downer while going on a date to Disneyland, and the objective is to meet the other person's excitement with high levels of disinterest as soon as you get to the park.

I know making a conscious effort to show how much less you can care than the other person is a defense mechanism that people utilize as a way of proceeding with caution and protecting themselves, but there's no real benefit. You should be transparent if you are expecting the same from the other person.

Purposely taking long to respond to texts, waiting an extra day to return calls, being nonchalant and whatever about spending time together- these things will only fill the other person with doubt. How can you tell if you are giving any opportunity to make a connection when you are allowing a wall between you? If it doesn't work out because you've offered only a part of your emotional self, you will need more time to bounce back. You will always have more questions. "Would things be different if they knew how I felt?" Imagine if your favorite shoe store had each pair of shoes wrapped in bubble wrap and placed on the shelf. They may be protected, but no one could see their real beauty.

> Stephen M.R. Covey says: "We judge ourselves by our intentions and others by their behavior."

When someone likes you and you're not feeling them, or maybe it's not the right time, it's easier to deliver excuses than it would be to potentially hurt their feelings by straightforwardly saying you're not interested, but what happens when the situation is reversed? When you turn the tables and they aren't returning your phone calls or always seem to be busy? Then, we're quick to wag our finger and claim it's about honesty and not giving false hope or blowing you off because, where is the respect in that?

We have all had times where we were hypocritical and dating tends to bring out at least two sides in all of us. You can be honest and not be wicked. There are ways to tell the truth without breaking someone's spirit. All you can do is control you and expect the same. When you're dealing with romance, someone's let down can be someone else's blessing.

Be honest and communicate your strengths and the strengths that you are looking for in a potential mate. If you don't feel you have any strengths or aren't sure because the relationships you've had thus far haven't ended up in marriage, you may need to start there.

Find an equal whose strengths compliment yours for today and for what you need for tomorrow. Keep in mind that equal, doesn't always mean a mirror image of what you are. If you are ambitious, having a man with the same qualities, which makes him equally ambitious, may create friction, leading to two strong willed people who can't stop arguing. Two people who demand attention, and two people who put their jobs before their relationships, which may be fine while you are starting in your career, but what about when you are in that career and one of you wants to slow down to have a family? What you may actually want is a guy who is a leader, in some areas, not necessarily in the boardroom. The traits you see in some of the men who are married may be great, but what you aren't looking at are the traits of the people they marry.

If you see yourself as an 'A-type' personality and you are attracted to alpha males who are ambitious, competitive, leaders and are opinionated. Ask yourself what they would get from dating you. The world revolves around them at their offices. He likes intellectually stimulating conversations, challenges and being celebrated for coming in to save the day. He always feels like he has to be 'on', coming up with all of the new ideas. But this is what he gets each day. What he can't get at work is nurturing, support, and intimacy to let his guard down. You may be able to provide some of that, but you are not going to be the easiest -going personality, always pushing because you think you know what's best, and he may want his life at home to be easy and be able to turn off. You want a guy who can lead, but who can also give you your way and let you lead. This combination may create conflict.

You have to decide what you want more. Do you want to keep dating the type of guys who have the qualities you have gone for in the past, even though it hasn't seemed to work or do you want to sit down and decide what are your wants versus your needs?

The guy may be totally wrong for you, but you owe it to yourself to go on a few dates and share some honest information about each other before you make a choice. If you didn't feel a sense of danger or a wave of nausea, dig a bit deeper to find out if there's an interest.

Don't let your fear of being without companionship prevent you from the small insecurities that will get you your reward. I learned to thrive at something I first feared when practicing hurdles for several years. When you educate and train yourself to know how to handle the jump and the fall, you become less fearful of falling. I remember running behind a grocery store, from a group of kids screaming racial slurs, when I first started practicing hurdles, and I used what I learned on the track to successfully out run the bullies, without getting hurt. Many of the hurdlers I admired genuinely had no fear of ever falling, because they knew their reflexes would just take over. Their whole body knew what to do. Somewhere around the time I reached my sophomore year in High School, I started experiencing this as well, almost wanting to jump over something higher just to see how my body would react from all the conditioning. I found out from other hurdlers that this is very common. When you know what to do, you not only stop being afraid, you actually begin to welcome the object of your fear. I'm not suggesting that inviting all of your fears is a good idea. I'm suggesting practice is a way to learn and education is a powerful way to destroy fear. Uncertainty breeds fear, but knowledge kills it.

You're unlikely to fear what you're good at, so a great way to conquer a fear is to make the commitment to practicing and mastering whatever it is you fear. This way you take control of the object of your fear by facing it in baby sized confrontations. Date and go home by yourself. Learn how to get knowledge by asking questions early. You won't ask someone all in one phone call; you're not a drill sergeant, or a snoop. Gain the knowledge by asking a few questions that will get to their relationship goals and values.

Men and women think differently. They also communicate differently. It is rare for men to lay out their cards upfront, so we need to ask the questions. We all get tired of finding someone and then realizing they aren't what they say they are.

Don't give yourself up before you know who you are dealing with. Ask the questions to get the information and then decide if it serves you to share yourself with him. Ask him in the same way you would question your girls when they call to tell you about their new man. You hear the eagerness in their voices, see past the fluff, laugh a little, and ask the same question in a different way to see if her answer will be the same. This isn't something you should do in one phone call, like an interrogation. Take your time.

Put your emotions and romantic notions aside and approach it with your head. Many people aren't willing to be honest if they aren't vested, and why would you want a man who isn't investing in you? Don't take your leverage off the table by putting your panties on the floor. It's like putting seasoning on a chicken while it's still wrapped. They don't taste the most important part.

Bob Marley said, "Everyone will hurt you, but you have to decide who is worth suffering for." You are the only one who can make a decision on what you can deal with or what you're signing up for. You will only be able to make a good decision if you have good information. You can only get good information when you get to the truth.

# *SAMMIES & WIENERS*

## YOU GET NA'AN

Serves: 1 sandwich

- 2 soft whole pita or naan bread
- ½ avocado
- 1 tablespoon basil pesto* (see below)
- roasted red bell pepper
- cucumber, sliced into thin rounds
- thinly sliced red onion
- 6 pitted Kalamata olives, thinly sliced
- handful spring salad mix
- balsamic vinegar

Pit and peel the avocado half and mash it with a fork. Use a butter knife to spread avocado on one slice of pita. Spread a layer of pesto (see below) on the other slice of bread.

Top the avocado bread with a single layer of roasted red bell pepper. Then add a layer of cucumber slices, red onion, olives and spring salad mix. Use a spoon to sprinkle some balsamic vinegar over the lettuce. Place the pesto slice on top, pesto side down.

This basic recipe is easy to make in bulk. Simply multiply the amounts provided below based by how many cups of basil you have. Freeze the leftover pesto for later!

*Pesto*

- 1 lightly packed cup of basil
- 1 garlic clove, peeled
- ¼ cup walnuts, lightly toasted
- ¼ cup extra-virgin olive oil (my food processor can't take any more oil and I felt like this was plenty)
- Sea salt, to taste
- squeeze of lemon juice

Over medium high heat, toast the walnuts until fragrant, about three to five minutes.

In a food processor, combine the basil, walnuts and garlic.

Pulse while drizzling in the olive oil.

Remove the mixture from the processor and pour it into a bowl. Stir in salt and a squeeze of lemon (optional), to taste.

## VEGAN CARROT "Hot Dogs"
Serves: 2 "hot dogs"

- 2 large carrots, peeled, with the ends cut off to the size of the hot dog bun
- 1/4 cup Coconut Liquid Aminos (I stay away from soy sauce & prefer this to Bragg's)
- 1/4 cup water
- 1 Tablespoon seasoned rice vinegar
- 1 Tablespoon sesame oil
- 1/2 Tablespoon apple cider vinegar
- dash liquid smoke
- 1 clove garlic, minced
- 1/4 tsp dried ginger
- 1/4 tsp black pepper
- 1/8 tsp granulated onion powder
- olive oil cooking spray
- 2 of your favorite hot dog buns
- desired hot dog toppings

Boil carrots for approximately 6 to 8 minutes, or until fork tender but *not soft/mushy*.

While the carrots are cooking, whisk together the Liquid Aminos, water, vinegars, sesame oil, liquid smoke, garlic, and seasonings.

After removing the carrots from the boiling water, run them under cold water to stop the cooking process.

Combine the carrots and the marinade in a zipper gallon-size bag (2 is suggested in case of a leak), or in an air-tight container. Shake gently until the carrots are coated with the marinade. Place the carrots in the refrigerator for at least 24 hours.

To 'grill' the carrots, spray a medium skillet with olive oil cooking spray. Turn the heat to medium and place the carrots and about 1/2 cup of the marinade into the non-still skillet/on a foil covered grill. Heat the carrots for approximately 8 to 10 minutes, or until warm.

The carrots get a nice crispy and seasoned coating on them from the marinade. This also helps give the "hot dogs" a more brown/tan color than their original orange color.

Serve your carrot "hot dogs" in a bun and top them with your favorite hot dog toppings.

## A COUPLE HOT DOGS
Yields: 4 large dogs/brats

*Spice Mix:*

- 1 ½ teaspoon garlic powder
- 1 teaspoon fennel, crushed
- ½ teaspoon black pepper
- ½ teaspoon salt
- 1 teaspoon sweet paprika
- 1 teaspoon smoked paprika
- ½ tsp. oregano
- ½ teaspoon red pepper flakes
- 1/8 teaspoon allspice

*Sausage*:

- 2 teaspoons olive oil
- 1 cup Portobello mushrooms, chopped
- ¼ cup onion, finely chopped
- 1 garlic clove, minced
- 2 cups or 1-15 oz. BPA-free can of black-eyed peas drained and rinsed
- 1 Tbs. sun-dried tomato paste
- ¼ cup nutritional yeast
- ½ cup brown rice flour
- 1 teaspoon ground chia/fax seed mixed w/ 2 teaspoons boiling water, mixed to a slush
- 2 Tablespoons gluten-free Worchester Sauce
- Few drops of liquid smoke (optional)

Prepare spice mix in advance. Set aside.

Heat a skillet with 2 tsp. of olive oil. Sauté the onions, mushrooms and garlic until softened. Set aside and let cool.

In a large bowl, add the black-eyed peas and mash them up. You can use a fork, a potato masher or your hands. * If you want to use a food processor, do a rough chop. You don't want a puree. Then add the tomato paste, nutritional yeast, and brown rice flour. Mix well.

Mix the chia/flax slurry and incorporate it well.

Add the cooled veggie mixture to the bowl and mix it into the dry ingredients. Add the Vegan Worcestershire Sauce to the bowl and mix it all up well. If you are using the Liquid Smoke, add it in now too.

Divide the mixture into 4 parts. Shape each part into a log. Wrap the logs individually in parchment paper & foil and steam them for 15-20 minutes. I use a metal steamer from my rice cooker. Then refrigerate for a few hours or overnight, if possible. This will help them firm up even more.

When ready to use, unwrap and cook them however you desire. Add your favorite condiments-Yum!!!

## CAN'T GET NONE OF MY FATTY PATTY
Yields: 4 patties

- 1-15 oz. BPA- free can black-eyed peas, drained and rinsed (or 1 ½ cups fresh cooked)
- 1 Tablespoons ground flax mixed with 3 Tbs. water, to slurry
- 1 cup cooked quinoa
- 1 small bell pepper, diced
- 3 scallions, finely sliced
- 1 clove garlic, minced
- 2 Tablespoon fresh parsley, finely chopped
- 1 teaspoon dried thyme
- 1 teaspoon dried mustard powder
- Sea salt and pepper to taste
- 3 dashes hot sauce or to taste
- 1 tsp. gluten-free, vegan Worcestershire sauce/Coconut Aminos
- 1/3 – ½ cup chickpea flour
- 1 Tablespoons safflower oil

In a small bowl or cup, mix the ground flax with water and let sit for 5 minutes until it is a slurry gel. Mash 1 cup of the black-eyed peas with the flax gel in a large bowl until there are no more beans intact.

Add the brown rice, bell pepper, scallions, garlic, parsley, spices, hot sauce and Worcestershire sauce/Aminos to the bowl and mix until all the ingredients are well-combined. Add in the flour little by little, mixing well with your hands, until you have a good consistency. You want it dry enough so that the burgers will hold together but not so dry, there is no moisture left at all. Throw in the remaining whole black-eyed peas and gently mix them in so they stay intact. Do NOT form the patties. Place the entire lump of black-eyed pea burger mix into the refrigerator and chill for at least 30 minutes.

When you are ready to cook, remove the mixture from the fridge and make into patties. Divide the mixture into 4 patties.

Heat the oil in a large skillet over medium-high heat. Cook the patties until browned, about 5 minutes per side. Flip patties them carefully several times to ensure that the inside cooks while the outside doesn't burn. I love to top mine with Boss Sauce (below) & put on my favorite bun.

### BOSS SAUCE
Yields: ½ cup

- 1/4 cup onion, minced
- 2 cloves garlic, minced
- 1/4 cup vegan mayonnaise
- 2 Tbsp. extra-virgin olive oil
- 2 Tbsp. ketchup
- 1 Tbs. Dijon mustard
- 1 Tbs. chili sauce, hot sauce or Siracha, or more to taste
- 1 Tbsp. vegan, Coconut Aminos/gluten-free Worcestershire sauce

- 1 Tbsp. fresh lemon juice
- 1 tsp prepared yellow mustard
- Sea salt and pepper to taste

Put all ingredients into a food processor and mix until smooth. Refrigerate in a covered container until ready to use. Use as a burger topping or a salad dressing.

## DO YOU FEEL-ME CHEESE STEAK
Yields: 4 sandwiches

- 2 teaspoons extra-virgin olive oil
- 1 medium onion, sliced
- 4 large Portobello mushrooms, stems and gills removed with spoon, sliced
- 1 large red bell pepper, thinly sliced
- 2 tablespoons minced fresh oregano, or 2 teaspoons dried
- 1/2 teaspoon freshly ground pepper
- 1 tablespoon all-purpose flour
- 1/4 cup vegetable broth
- 1 tablespoon coconut Aminos (Whole Foods)
- 3 ounces thinly sliced reduced-fat provolone cheese
- 4 favorite/gluten free Udi buns, split and toasted

Heat oil in a large nonstick skillet over medium-high heat. Add onion and cook, stirring often, until soft and beginning to brown, 3 minutes. Add mushrooms, bell pepper, oregano and pepper and cook, stirring often, until the vegetables are wilted and soft, about 7 minutes.

Reduce heat to low; sprinkle the vegetables with flour and stir to coat. Stir in broth and Coconut Aminos sauce; bring to a simmer. Remove from the heat, lay cheese slices on top of the vegetables, cover and let stand until melted, 1 to 2 minutes.

Divide the mixture into 4 portions with a spatula, leaving the melted cheese layer on top. Scoop a portion onto each toasted bun and serve immediately.

## SPICY CHICKPEA SALAD (Vegan)
Serves: 2 to 3

- 1 15 oz can chickpeas, drained and rinsed well
- 1 stalk celery, finely diced
- 3 organic baby carrots, finely diced
- 2 teaspoons dried onion flakes
- 2 Tablespoons vegan mayo (I use the Earth Balance brand)* (or reg mayo if you aren't vegan)
- 2 Tablespoons vegan ranch dressing*
- 2 to 4 tsp buffalo sauce (depending on how spicy you like your food)
- Serve on Romaine hearts, or your favorite bread

Combine all ingredients in a medium bowl and stir until well-combined.

Refrigerate for at least 3-4 hours, or until chilled.

## *No Yo' MAYO (Vegan)*

Yields: 1 ½ cups

- 1/2 cup hemp/coconut milk
- 1/2 teaspoon sea salt
- 1 teaspoon ground mustard
- 2 teaspoons garlic powder
- 2 teaspoons apple cider vinegar
- 2 teaspoons agave
- 1 cup organic canola oil

Place soy milk, sea salt, ground mustard, garlic powder, vinegar and agave in a blender. Place the lid on the blender and turn to slow.

Take the middle part of the blender's lid out while the blender is still running and slowly pour in the canola oil.

Place the lid back on and blend until the mayo is thick and creamy.

## *VEGAN RANCH*

- 1 cup No Yo Mayo
- 1/2 teaspoon garlic powder
- 1/2 teaspoon onion powder
- 1/4 teaspoon black pepper
- 2 teaspoons parsley, chopped
- 1/2 cup unsweetened coconut milk

Whisk all ingredients together and chill before serving. Add a little more coconut milk if you need to thin dressing.

## NACHO USUAL VEGAN CHEESE (Vegan)
Serves: 6

- 2 cups peeled, boiled, and mashed potatoes (requires about 2 - 2 1/2 medium potatoes) *when butternut squash is in season I use half & half
- 3/4 cups peeled, chopped, and boiled carrots (I used 2 large peeled carrots cut in 1 inch pieces)
- ½ jalapeno, diced sautéed
- 1/2 cup nutritional yeast flakes
- 1/3 cup extra virgin olive oil
- ¼ teaspoon garlic powder
- 1/3 cup water
- 1 tablespoon lemon juice
- 1 1/2 teaspoon sea salt

Boil your potatoes and carrots until they are fork tender, then measure them into your blender. Make sure your potatoes are mashed/packed into your measuring cups. The carrots can be loosely measured.

Place all ingredients in your blender.

Blend on high for about 30 seconds, or until mixture is completely smooth.

Serve immediately with chips, or dribble over veggies. Refrigerate leftovers in an airtight container for up to 1 week. Reheat leftovers on low on the stove (stirring constantly) or in the microwave for 35 seconds to 1 minute.

# ONE MAN'S STORY, ANOTHER WOMAN'S STEW

In the famed words of Eartha Kitt, "A man's first job should be to pick you up, not lay you down."

I can look back on every bad choice and say, "God showed me a sign." He gave me a voice inside of myself, and sometimes I need to be still to hear it. Some people choose to call it intuition. The more you use your intuition, the more you build trust in your intuitive insight, and the more you're able to follow your intuition and you can identify crazy and cross the street.

My last relationship was six years, but hardly worth mentioning. I am summing it up that way because I felt betrayed and blindsided.

The break up was hasty and ugly. There were broken things and broken promises. My sons were also part of the casualties; disappointed after they had opened their hearts and trying their best to understand what having a father-son relationship meant. I felt like I had let them down and sat down to reflect on my role in the decision to be in this relationship. I realized I bail when I feel threatened and tested. You can't blend anything when there's resistance from either element. I don't want to rehearse my history, but I chalked the ending as a lesson to grow from, knowing forgiveness is a gift we should give ourselves.

However despite my best efforts, I was looking at divorce-heartbroken, crying into my down comforter at night-and my keyboard in the middle of the day. As if my private misery wasn't enough, I braced myself for the reactions on Facebook when I updated my relationship status (waiting until 3 o'clock in the morning). I dreaded from the pit of my ice-cream-and-wine-filled stomach the torrent of "OMG what happened?" and ":("from people I barely knew, and even worse, the congratulations from people who never liked my ex in the first place.

I had to endure months of emotional anguish and layers of barriers in order to put my house in order and give my boys a sense of home. Twelve hours before we were to appear in court for our dissolution, he came to my office to make an announcement to me that he had changed his mind and didn't want to lose me. Over those months it became clear he and I didn't have the same values. I have always gone into a relationship understanding there are rough patches and needs to compromise, but there is a difference between being 'realistic' and being with the wrong person. The one glaring thing that stood out to me was the ugliness and disrespect he displayed while ending it in front of the kids. I had to admit to myself that the Band-Aid the ex and I were going to attempt to put on our relationship wasn't going to hold. There's no Facebook option for "exes in denial."

The fishbowl experience of Facebook and other social media profiles seems in contradiction to the seeming trend of being noncommittal-to career paths, to jobs, to relationships. Many people live their lives out online, on full display, but they also want the freedom to change their minds every few days, to have ambiguous relationships and embrace what's been labeled as the "hook-up culture." I've never been comfortable with that. I haven't been enticed or curious to try on-line dating or match-making services.

I was reserved to prayer and never marrying again. Then, God stepped in (He really never left, but it had to be divine intervention.) and I found that I met the "right one" a long time ago. There will be more on that later.

In discussing the pluses and minuses with relationship's impact on social media, I wanted to get more feedback regarding on-line dating and why people would choose to meet someone based on a profile they read on line. I wasn't interested in hedging my bets, after realizing I dismissed a good guy for a bad reason. I wanted to hear how a person, who seems great based on a profile, could turn out to be as disappointing as often as the guy you write off as not being your type turns out to be appealing.

"I hadn't met anyone organically, and I didn't want to go out looking for someone, putting my singleness out in the streets," Tina, an extremely attractive PhD and administrator at a University chimed in. "If she's so great, why isn't she with someone?" Is what people say, and you walk away not sure if it's a compliment or an insult. So I decided, if I was looking and the guys were posting on-line, it didn't seem as bad.

"I tend to go for guys that say things like, "I want a woman who is independent and has her own interests." This, I've only recently understood, means, *I only have time for women who are as responsive as my smart phone, has the sexual disposition of a video vixen, who is also captain of a twerk team.* I also tend to go out with guys who write 'Communication is key,' to answer the question, 'What I Learned From My Last Relationship'-an asinine category which should be re-titled, 'What I Definitely Did Not Learn From My Last Relationship Otherwise I'd Still Be In It.' I've come to understand these guys would rather join the military, during wartime, rather than have a conversation about the relationship and where we are headed. The end result of this conversation being, "Nowhere and Fast".

To be fair, men also have profound and reflective complaints about the females online; namely, false advertising. Women often lie about their weight and age. I know this because they've told me. That's what people do who visit dating chat sites. They talk about other dating sites like they are at a family reunion and they are trying to catch up with cousins they haven't seen in years. Even though it's more like we're at casting calls for a new reality show, staring us, and trying to come up with the best or worst story lines.

Tina continued, "But I've found, as someone who has been on about fifty first dates in the last two years, it's not the worst stories that get to you; not the guy who tries to run his fingers through your freshly coifed weave while kissing you 'because you've been tossing it all evening, so I thought you'd like it'; or the hottie who, in the middle of the date, accidentally texts you, 'Date's not going too well'; or the one who reveals he's an environmentalist as he wraps up your food, as well as the people at the table behind us, because he needs it for his compost.

No, it's the huge amount of people who are not for you, and if they paid the slightest bit of attention, they wouldn't have wasted my time. The guy who looks exactly like his picture but who has as much chemistry as a paper plate; the one who sits across from you after he liked the picture of me in my Greek logo embroidered sweater that he thinks all sorority girls pay to have friends; the one who orders the crab cakes and offers you a bite even though you stated in your profile that you are deathly allergic to shell fish. I'm not saying there is anything wrong with any of these people per se, if per se means 'for someone else.'

Besides, that dating site owes me. Yes, that's right. *SinglesMingle.com* owes me a husband. I've paid them more than a thousand dollars, not to mention at least two hundred hours of dating time, which doesn't include my prep time for pedicures, waxing and retail. If dating were tax deductible, I could write off a quarter of my life. Ergo, I must meet someone on *SinglesMingle*."

Beth, a 33 year old talent manager added, "There is a saying amongst women trying to date from a LinkedIn 'professional' meet up: The odds are good, but the goods are odd. There are tons of guys, but they tend to be socially awkward, career-obsessed, and prone to a never grow old, *life is a party* mentality.

If you are in an average income bracket, with a relatively good title, or above average looking female, finding a date isn't an issue. You have several guys you can go on dates with, but what makes it difficult is finding a viable partner.

Lots of men can be socially awkward. They are extremely smart, some entrepreneurial, and logical and who think, 'I can apply those practices to a relationship and my rational logic can be applied the same way.' They don't realize that as women, we can be emotional - and a lot of guys don't have tolerance for that," she summarized.

"Many guys have the mentality that they'll wait and they'll find the perfect woman. They don't realize that relationships aren't about perfection. They often choose work over relationships because; it's all black and white. They say they love their jobs because it's about fixing a problem and there is always a solution. They don't realize that this isn't how it works in real life," Tina added.

I decided to bring in a group of men and women to see how easy it would be to judge what people put on a profile given that men and women tend to want different things. Women tend to have a concrete picture in their minds of what 'Mr. Right' will be like. Men have a vaguer notion and don't dive so deeply into the details. I've also heard that women tend to make more calculated decisions than men do. I don't know if this tends to be because women grow up imagining who would be there to help them raise their children. Each gender had different expectations. Women may not be willing to give a man a chance at a date for fear of settling, but men aren't going to settle for a wife. Which decision has more of an impact?

The amount of people participating in on-line dating services has increased. Internet profiles make what you're looking for seem objective, when actual connection to someone is very subjective. The less you know about your potential 'match' before you meet the better. Just because he says he likes Bob Marley or Snoop Lion doesn't mean he prefers flip flops to Ferragamos and spends his evenings smoking weed. The profiles don't leave much room for the fantasy to build.

When you know too much about a person before seeing them, it makes it harder to become interested in them. Eli J. Finkel, a psychology professor in the Self Control & Relationship Lab at Northwestern did a study showing that people don't actually know what traits they want in a partner. People can tell you what they like, but not why. For example; saying, "I am attracted to this man," could be an accurate statement. You ARE attracted to him. However, my girlfriend explains further stating, "It's because he makes money." This might not be an accurate explanation. It could be closer for her to say, "It is because he is generous." Your must-haves and your deal breakers are the "what", when they should be the "why."

After sitting through a few panel discussions on male and female relationships, I decided to write down my absolute needs rather than my wants. I started a process to create what I wanted, instead of being upset about what I didn't have. My want list had about twelve essential items. It seemed a bit mentally exhaustive to keep up with. I wasn't sure if that meant if a guy only had eleven of the twelve I had to let him go. I decided I would not have more than three. I have learned that what you want isn't necessarily good for you, and when going after the person you think you want, you tend to ignore what you really need. Distinguishing wants from needs can be confusing. I needed some more clarity. I looked up wants and needs on a search engine.

NEED: something you have to have.

WANT: something you would like to have.

I was able to narrow down to these essential needs: intellectually curious, enjoys kids, believes in God, and financially stable; which meant no debt, to me. I had other qualities I was looking for, but this is what someone would have to have in order for me to go on a date. In other words, I couldn't rule him out based on the car he drove or his title. I would give it a chance at a date if we talked and he met these four requirements. I knew this wasn't a magic formula, but it seemed better than becoming emotionally unavailable and more hopeful than resolving in my bitterness and never letting another man close to me. I was making progress.

# *JERKS, CHICKENS, MEATLOAFS & LIMP NOODLES*

## JERK CHICKEN

*Jerk Sauce*

- 1/2 cup malt vinegar (or white vinegar)
- 2 Tbsp dark rum (optional)
- 2 Scotch bonnet peppers (or habaneros), with seeds, chopped
- 1 red onion, chopped
- 4 green onion tops, chopped
- 1 Tablespoons dried thyme or 2 Tbsp fresh thyme leaves, chopped
- 1 Tablespoon olive oil
- 2 teaspoons salt
- 2 teaspoons freshly ground black pepper
- 4 teaspoons ground allspice (I prefer to start with whole allspice & grind in coffee grinder)
- 2 teaspoons ground cinnamon
- 4 teaspoons ground nutmeg
- 4 teaspoons ground ginger

- ½ cup of brown sugar (adds sweetness & helps smoke when on grill)
- 2 teaspoons molasses
- 1 (5 or 6 pound) roasting chicken, cut in halves, lengthwise
- 1/2 cup lime juice
- 1/3 cup melted coconut oil
- Salt and pepper
- Bay leaves and whole pimento soaked in water

Marinate overnight (at least 4 hours) to seal in flavor and prevent dryness. Preheat oven to 350°F. Place chicken halves in a rimmed baking pan, skin side up. Roast on a bed of bay leaves which have been soaked in water until chicken halves are cooked through, about 50-60 minutes. The chicken is done when the juices run clear (not pink) when a knife tip is inserted into both the chicken breast and thigh, about 165-170°F for the breast and 180-185°F for the thigh. Transfer chicken to plate.  *when grilling, I soak pimento wood & place chicken on top, I also throw water soaked pimentos on the coals, cooking on cooler side of coals. Finish last 5 minutes on hot side of grill.  If you can't find pimento, try hickory & cherry wood) Serve with rice & peas cabbage & corn.


## VEGGIE JERK
Serves: 4

- 2 red onion, 1 diced, 1 roughly chopped
- 2 tablespoons of sunflower oil
- 50 g fresh ginger chopped
- Small bunch of coriander, leaves & stalks separated
- 2 thyme sprigs
- 1 teaspoon of allspice*
- 1 teaspoon nutmeg*
- ½ teaspoon of cinnamon*
- ¼ teaspoon cloves
- ½ teaspoon sea salt*
- ½ teaspoon of black pepper*

- ½ teaspoon minced garlic*
- 1 teaspoon chipotle chili powder*
- 400g BPA-free cans diced tomatoes
- 4 tablespoons of red wine vinegar
- tablespoons of organic brown sugar
- organic vegetable stock cubes
- 6 sweet potatoes, peeled & cut into chunks
- 2 400g BPA free cans of black beans, rinsed & drained
- large roasted red peppers cut into thick slices

Saute the diced onion in the sunflower oil in deep a non-stick pan. Whisk together the chopped onion, ginger, coriander stalks and jerk seasonings* with a hand held blender. Add the sauted onion and fry until fragrant.

Stir in the thyme, diced tomatoes, vinegar, sugar, and stock cubes with 3 cups water, and bring to a simmer. Simmer for 10 minutes, then add sweet potatoes and simmer an additional 10 minutes. Stir in the beans, peppers and some seasoning, and simmer 5 minutes until the potatoes are almost tender. Cool. Add chopped coriander leaves and serve.

## BROWN STEW CHICKEN
Serves: 6

- 3 lbs Chicken, cut in pieces and skin removed

*Chicken Marinating Seasonings:*

- 2 teaspoon Sea Salt
- 1teaspoon apple cider vinegar/lemon juice
- 1teaspoon dried thyme
- 1/2 teaspoon Black pepper
- 2 teaspoon Sugar
- 3 Large cloves garlic, minced
- 2 stalk scallion (green onion) chopped

*Gravy:*

- 1/2 cup Cooking oil (for frying chicken)
- 1Large red onion, chopped
- 1/4 each, Red and Green bell pepper, chopped
- 1Sprig of thyme or 1teaspoon dried
- 2 small jalapenos seeded and chopped
- 2 small Roma tomatoes (diced)
- 1Tablespoon Tomato paste
- 2 cups Hot water
- 1teaspoon salt (to taste)

Season chicken with vinegar/lime juice, salt, black pepper, thyme, sugar, garlic and scallion (green onion). Marinate the chicken overnight of at least one hour before frying.

Shake off lose spices from chicken and, on High heat, fry the chicken in cooking oil for 2 to 3 minutes on each side, until browned. Remove chicken from pan, set aside.

Remove half the cooking oil in pan and use remaining oil to fry onions, jalapeno peppers, bell peppers until onions are transparent, add tomatoes and toss slightly.

Add thyme, tomato paste and 1cup of hot water to pan and stir; taste gravy and add 1tsp of sea salt, if needed.

Add chicken to tomato mixture. Add 1cup of hot water and turn heat to Low and cover pan. Simmer chicken for 30 minutes or until it is tender and the gravy has thickened. Serve with steamed rice, fried plantains or a salad.

## CHICK HOT TWEENST THE THIGHS
Serves: 6-8

- 3-3.5 lbs of organic chicken (boneless, skinless thighs)
- 1 tablespoon Apple cider vinegar
- ½ teaspoon cumin
- ½ teaspoon cayenne
- 1 teaspoon organic coriander
- 1 teaspoon organic paprika (smoked is preferred)
- 3 garlic cloves, minced
- ¼ teaspoon organic thyme
- ¼ teaspoon tumeric
- ¼ teaspoon sea salt
- ¼ teaspoon freshly ground black pepper

Preheat oven to 400 degrees F and line rimmed baking sheet with aluminum foil (sprayed with oil).
Cut chicken breasts into strips with a knife or kitchen scissors (very convenient for no cutting board cleanup).

I used 6 large chicken thighs that I cut into 3 strips each lengthwise. Place in a large bowl & toss in vinegar.

In a small bowl, combine spices ingredients and sprinkle on top of chicken. Toss chicken to coat evenly in spices. Lay in a single layer on prepared baking sheet and bake for 25-30 mins.

## CHICKEN WITH RUM COCONUT:
Serves 4:

- 12 chicken wings or small drumsticks
- 4 tablespoons butter
- 6 tablespoons refined organic coconut oil
- 4 to 6 tablespoons Jamaican rum
- 2 or 3 chicken bouillon cubes crushed
- Garlic powder; for seasoning
- Dash freshly ground black pepper
- 1 2/3 cups coconut cream
- 1 1/4 cups heavy cream
- 1/4 cup mushrooms (optional)
- 1/2 teaspoon thyme

Rinse the chicken wings and cut off and discard the small jointed fingerlike tips. Cut each wing in half to produce a flat part and fleshy mini-drumstick.

In a large, heavy-based pan, heat the butter and coconut oil. Sauté the chicken wings until golden brown and cooked. Depending on the size of your pan, you may have to fry in small batches. When all the chicken wings are cooked, return them to the pan on the stove and decrease the heat. This next part is tricky, so be careful. Quickly pour the rum over the chicken wings, and light a match to set the rum alight. Carefully tilt the pan to ensure all the chicken wings are flambéed.

When the flames die down, add the bouillon cubes, garlic powder, lots of pepper, the coconut cream, and the cream. Stir well to mix and simmer gently for 15 to 20 minutes. Add 1/4 cup mushrooms- optional and simmer on low to medium heat until the sauce thickens. Serve hot.

## TURKEY MEATLOAF

- 1 cup chopped yellow onions (1 large onion)
- ½ cup diced red/yellow peppers
- 2 tablespoons olive oil
- 2 teaspoons kosher salt
- 1 teaspoon freshly ground black pepper
- 1 teaspoon fresh thyme leaves (1/2 teaspoon dried)
- 1/4 cup Worcestershire sauce
- 1/4 cup chicken stock
- 1 1/2 teaspoons tomato paste
- 3 pounds ground grass-fed turkey breast
- 3/4 cups oatmeal
- 2 extra-large eggs, beaten
- 3/4 cup ketchup/barbeque sauce

Preheat oven to 325 degrees F.

In a medium sauté pan, over medium-low heat, cook the onions, olive oil, salt, pepper, and thyme until translucent, but not browned, approximately 10 minutes. Add the Worcestershire sauce, chicken stock, and tomato paste and mix well. Allow to cool to room temperature.

Combine the ground turkey, oatmeal crumbs, eggs, and onion mixture in a large bowl. Mix well and shape into a rectangular loaf on an ungreased sheet pan. Spread the ketchup evenly on top. Bake for 1

1/2 hours until the internal temperature is 160 degrees F. and the meatloaf is cooked through. (A pan of hot water in the oven under the meatloaf will keep the top from cracking.) Serve w/yams or potatoes & corn.

## BAYOU (BYE YOU!) NOODLES
Serves: 2

- 2 boneless skinless chicken breast halves, cut into thin strips
- 4 ounces linguine, cooked al dente  (I also use zucchini strips)
- 2 teaspoons cajun seasoning (Bayou Shake  Mix below or store-bought)
- 3 tablespoons sunflower oil
- 1 thinly sliced green onion
- can coconut milk  (full cream coconut)
- tablespoons chopped sun-dried tomatoes
- 1/4 teaspoon sea salt
- 1/4 teaspoon dried basil
- ½ small green pepper, chopped
- 1/8 teaspoon ground black pepper
- cloves garlic, minced
- ¼ cup fresh grated Parmesan cheese

Bring a large pot of lightly salted water to a boil. Add linguini pasta, and cook for 8 to 10 minutes, or until al dente; drain.

Meanwhile, place chicken and Bayou Shake seasoning in a bowl, and toss to coat.

In a large skillet over medium heat, saute chicken in sunflower oil until no longer pink and juices run clear, about 5 to 7 minutes. Add garlic, green pepper, and green onions; cook for 2 to 3 minutes. Reduce heat, and stir in heavy coconut cream. Season the sauce with basil, salt, and ground black pepper, and heat through.

In a large bowl, toss linguini with sauce. Sprinkle with grated Parmesan cheese.

*Bayou Shake*

- 2 teaspoons of sea salt
- 2 teaspoons garlic powder
- 2 1/2 teaspoons paprika
- 1 teaspoon ground black pepper
- 1 teaspoon onion powder

- 1 teaspoon cayenne pepper
- 1 1/4 teaspoons dried oregano
- 1 1/4 teaspoons dried thyme
- 1/2 teaspoon red pepper flakes (optional)

Store in airtight container.

*Nutritionists Jayson and Mira Calton are among those who say bone broth, from organic grass-fed meat is the original 'souper' food. The broth used from bones you may discard can create a health tonic with numerous benefits-it contains easily absorbable minerals like; calcium, silicon, sulphur and magnesium. The gelatin in bone broth assists digestion by attracting good 'belly' juices and has been shown to help heal prior damage to the gut lining, offering relief to those with digestive disorders. A bowl of broth also contains chondroitin sulfate, now famous as a supplement for osteoarthritic joint pain.

## *How can vegetarians get protein?*

### Lentils

Lentils, a small but nutritionally mighty member of the legume family, are a very good source of cholesterol-lowering fiber. Not only do lentils help lower cholesterol, they are of special benefit in managing blood-sugar disorders since their high fiber content prevents blood sugar levels from rising rapidly after a meal. **Protein: 18 grams, 1 cup cooked**

**Hempseed**

This hemp won't get anyone stoned. This relative of the popular narcotic contains significant amounts of all nine essential amino acids, as well as plenty of magnesium, zinc, iron, and calcium. They're also a rare vegan source of essential fatty acids, like omega-3s, which can help fight depression without the need to get high! **Protein: 10 grams per 2 tablespoon serving**

**Soy**

While beans are normally low in the amino acid methionine, soy is a complete protein and thoroughly deserves its status as the go-to substitute for the meat-free (stay away from processed varieties). Tempeh is made by fermenting the beans, but tofu is probably the best known soy product. If protein's a concern, it's important to choose the firmest tofu available—the harder the tofu, the higher the protein content. **Protein: 10 grams per ½ cup serving (firm tofu)**

**Quinoa**

Quinoa looks a lot like couscous, but it's way more nutritious. Full of fiber, iron, magnesium, and manganese, quinoa is a terrific substitute for rice and it's versatile enough to make muffins, fritters, cookies, and breakfast casseroles. **Protein: 8 grams per 1 cup serving, cooked**

**Buckwheat**

He was my favorite character from the Little Rascals-*not that one*. Buckwheat isn't a type of wheat at all, but a relative of rhubarb. Many cultures eat the seeds by either grinding them into flour (making a great base for gluten-free pancakes!) or cooking the hulled kernels, or "groats," similarly to oatmeal. Buckwheat is crazy healthy: Some studies have shown that it may improve circulation, lower blood cholesterol and control blood glucose levels. **Protein: 6 grams per 1 cup serving, cooked**

# GOOD INGREDIENTS VS FANCY PACKAGING

For men, it is crucial to understand that a woman who is independent and seemingly needing nothing, actually desires and needs quite a bit from you. She may not appear to need money, a vehicle, or someone to mow the grass (although she probably wouldn't mind if you volunteered every now and then), but wishes to have those things she can't provide for herself- love, respect, adoration, kindness, and companionship. Don't confuse independence for a sign telling men, "I don't *HAVE TO HAVE* anyone in my life to be happy"- because it doesn't translate to, "I wish to be alone."

For women, it is very important to understand and appreciate a man's natural dispositions. These human characteristics have been ingrained in men since creation, when God created Adam & said; "Be fruitful", man was tasked with hunting, braving the harsh elements and providing for family. Not only were men expected to do it, but they enjoyed doing it. Taking care of family gave a sense of accomplishment, which is one of the greatest achievements a man can experience.

There is an ongoing power struggle which is usually never addressed verbally and rarely does one actually claim victory (to their mate, that is). Power is fickle, hard to hold onto and a challenge to define. What is power? (Even physics can't answer the question. Power is simply defined circularly as "the ability to do work.") In love, the tables can turn rapidly and without warning.

Power is inconsistent and there are ways to have power without appearing to have it. Men, if you really want power, well, you already have it. It's been in your hands all along, just waiting for you to use it. The same is true of women. Each one of us has the potential to be both powerless and incredibly powerful, maybe even at the same time.

Women have a great deal of power, more power than we can imagine. Since puberty, men have made 95% of their decisions based on the wishes of the holders of the Double X Chromosome. How we dress, act, walk, talk, move, pose, work, laugh, compete, and conquer relates to the golden pursuit…women.

Women have driven men, from age 14 to 102. Sure, men are driven by their work, but most men will also agree that their pursuit of work is directly related to their pursuit of women or providing for the woman in their lives. Men have always found the ultimate gratification in being able to provide for a woman (and their families). When they were hunters and gatherers, they would spend all day, sometimes two, traveling the area with spears in hand, hunting down mighty game to literally bring home the bacon (turkey bacon) to a woman's accepting hands. There are thousands of years of history of male/female relations pumping through our DNA and if we stop to examine this history, we can find much success in the present day.

Power, however, is a dangerous tool to wield. Both men and women have their own distinctive powers, but the goal is not to seek to have power over others. Wielding power over others often hurts the wielder more than anyone else. My message is one of self-empowerment. In general, as you are dating, women are empowered by being selective and keeping just enough mystery that men have to work for their respect.

Men, your empowerment comes from selection. Think of it this way. You have the opportunity to choose from all the ladies you know or, at least, from the ones in the room with you, to ask one for a date, a dance or an opportunity to get to know each other. Don't think of it as a risk at rejection. If you get rejected, brush your shoulders off, assume you are saving yourself from someone who wasn't right for you and ask someone else.

Contrary to what you may think, a man's sex organ is not in his pants but in his eyes. They are extremely visual. It is said that men are turned on through their eyes while women are turned on through their ears. Scientifically speaking, men have an innate relationship with every aspect of your body, from the curve of your back, to the whiteness of your eyes, to the adornment of your hair. Chemicals charge a man's system every time women do something as simple as whip their hair or let their fingers glide across their neck. Nature wants men to continue the human race and is constantly trying to provoke a man to pursue a woman.

Whether we like it or not, power is at the heart of all our relationships. It is impossible to have a meaningful relationship with someone without having some power over that person, and he or she must also have some power over you. The problem is, power corrupts, and in order for relationships to survive, a balance must be found to temper that potential corruption.

Many marriage counselors will share that the presence of contempt in the speech or demeanor of one marital partner is a sign that the relationship is doomed. There is no room for contempt and love to occupy the same space for a length of time; one will have to give way.

In part, it emerges from the power that one person in a relationship has over the other. Power is having control over the things that other people need and want It is also having power over what they fear. It is toxic when one person uses control over the thing that the other desires – affection, or the thing the other fears – abandonment. The desire to love and be loved is the most basic human need for both genders.

A group of my friends, and other diners, were standing in the tasting room at Cooper's Hawk, waiting to be seated. As we sipped samples of wine and tasted delicious morsels of chocolate sweets, while chatting with new acquaintances, gradually the general conversation seemed to die out, withering as we all noticed the particular interaction between two of the guests.

It was somehow as if the rest of us weren't there, and she acted almost if she were alone in the room with the forlorn-looking man who, with downcast eyes, was already sinking another drink.

If this had been a workplace, she wouldn't have stood a chance – harassment, bullying, mental cruelty – any judge or tribunal would have nailed her. It was a scene out of *Real Housewives, Love and No Hope"*, a public humiliation in front of strangers. A systematic dismantling of his qualities; personal, professional, looks, social, intellectual – and yes, even two years later I feel the excruciating embarrassment at the memory – oblique hints of sexual inadequacies too. They were both wearing rings. This man appeared to be her husband.

Razaaq– not his real name – took it like a whipped dog. The more he took it, the more strangely enlivened she looked; her eyes glittered, her voice rose and her viciousness deepened. She exuded triumph and something much worse – contempt.

Whatever the battle she was fighting, Whitney – not her real name – was clearly the winner of this contest. Her whole bright-eyed demeanor was that of the victor, like a gladiator occasionally glancing around at us, as if we were spectators expected to give the thumbs up or down to this poor loser's mental life.

So she had this considerable emotional power over him, but why should that make her feel contempt for him? Research out of Stanford University suggests one possible reason. If we arouse power feelings in otherwise ordinary people, they begin to see others as objects.

The research showed that when students were primed with power, by reliving a situation from their past, where they had power over someone, they were also inclined to see others in terms of how useful they were to them. In other words, it wasn't an issue they could point to that made them feel contempt, it was the level at which they felt the person had something they needed.

Once you start to see others as objects, whose actions are under your control, it is very easy to start to feel contempt for them. Objects, after all, don't have free will and don't make decisions. This sort of power extinguishes empathy. How can we have empathy for an object?

It was clear that 'Whitney' had no empathy for 'Razaaq's humiliation – if anything she seemed to be reveling in it. I had no idea of their history, but to wait and do this in a public place showed no responsibility over emotions and it seemed to play out like a game. However, the lack of empathy, even cruelty, doesn't equate to contempt. We all stood looking at each other, wondering what makes a person yield their 'power' in such a public display.

I try to be very mindful over my tongue, because I believe there are two things you can't take back once put into the atmosphere; a bullet and your words. I have been objectified, while on the receiving end of someone's loose mouth, and my reaction has been to avoid getting into a spar of words and to refrain from hitting below the belt. I have learned that I need to be mindful of timing and have clear foundation on what each person sees as emulating respect and displaying submissiveness.

As Whitney's emotional power over Razaaq made her see him an object under her control, her behavior deteriorated. It was clear that Whitney saw herself as a decent, liberal-minded person, and that led to dissension between how she saw herself and her actions. As people are strongly motivated to reduce discord, then her mind unconsciously did so by developing contempt for

Whitney which was more in accord with the humiliating way she was treating him.

Whitney was not a psychologically disturbed person, prone to cruelty throughout her life. No, she and her husband had descended into a situation where she held all the cards in their relationship. She had total emotional power and that power led her into the belief that she was a winner in this strange emotional battle.

Razaaq's body language, of course, began to show the symptoms of extreme powerlessness – slacked shoulders, no eye contact (obviously from embarrassment). Having been in a similar situation, I can imagine it soon elevated to passivity, loss of initiative, depression, decreased enthusiasm to go home (which will lead to other issues), fearfulness over losing his children and hopelessness. This is not an attractive package for any partner- male or female. Nobody gets hot for a loser. Whitney's power and careless behavior towards Razaaq caused his broken spirit to retreat into defenselessness. The careless rate at which he was drinking simply confirmed the rationalization of her extraordinary behavior. It encouraged her to see him as someone who couldn't respectfully take charge of the situation leading to her contempt for him.

It may seem strange that I chose an example of female on male abuse when I have experienced domestic violence, and worldwide many more women are victims of unequal power than are men. Men are not systematically deprived of human rights such as the right to education or limitations in the workforce, by political and religious systems because of their gender. On the other hand, this is an occurrence, in many countries, for women. The resulting powerlessness of hundreds of millions of women can fundamentally shape their view of self-value, reducing their capacity to change their situation.

I chose Whitney and Razaaq because it made the story of their behavior easier to tell than if it had been a male to female abuse story. Had it been a tale of Razaaq publicly humiliating Whitney, we (mainly speaking of women who are reading this book) may have been dismissive and it may well have unconsciously primed our minds to images of males inevitably dominating women because of inherited biological drives over which women have reduced control.

What I discovered, from feedback from both sexes, during the writing of this book is that women want men who want to grow their relationship, as much as they want to grow themselves. Men want women to understand they can and should have courage to ask for what they want, with understanding that we need to be responsible for our emotional experience and expression. Men want a woman who displays a need for them out of want, not desperation. The best way for each party to get what they want is with sugar, not salt.

It is part of a man's wiring to provide for you. Most of his self-esteem and gratification emanated from success in bringing home the food or the paycheck to his lady. Women must see that a man is not the only one capable of providing and protecting. This point is even more powerful today. Since a man's ability to flex his provisional muscle is not as dominant as it once was, before the two-person income and the elevation of women in the workplace, a woman can take note on how to build him up by finding creative ways in to let him provide for you.

Another part of a man's wiring is in protecting. This is similar to the concept of providing. Men feel most proud when they feel like they can be your mighty shield. There is a certain mix of a woman's confidence, sprinkled with a touch of power, in acting shy, reserved, and coy. How does this work? I like to think of it in terms of a woman's 'cookie' or goodies. The term *cookie* gained popularity from Steve Harvey's *Think Like A Man* series of books. In the context of this book I will ask you to imagine yourself getting out the ingredients to bake a batch of cookies, but unknowingly you have mixed up the salt and the sugar. You end up putting in a cup of salt and a dash of sugar. Now picture a little child taking a big bite out of those cookies. How long will it take the child to realize something is wrong? Do you think he or she will ask for another cookie? Of course not!

The art of seasoning is a matter of balance; just enough salt to notice, but not too much to overwhelm. Salt creates a thirst, a desire for more, but it takes a very small amount. Sugar keeps people coming back. They are drawn to it.

Does it work to make a man feel needed? Yes, because it insights a man's intuitive nature to protect. I am not suggesting that you put on a show of coyness and reservation? If that is not your style, there are other ways to elicit his protective nature. Even though you can protect yourself and take care of the situation, men will melt and feel appreciated when they feel like you adore their protection and presence; that they are your knight in shining armor.

One thing that I think women don't realize is that men find a woman's submissiveness, not only a huge turn on, but in reality, a woman's submissiveness holds its own kind of strength. It's a different type of strength. In the same way that many women crave a strong man to lead them, men crave women who are strong in their fearlessness when it comes to embracing their femininity and in being submissive.

I used to see submission as a threat to my personal power. Then I realized my intimidation came from fear and past pain. Submission requires vulnerability and trust in the partner, a yielding of authority. I realized that the problem I was having with submission really had nothing to do with the concept but rather the men with whom I dealt. It was easy to submit to my mentors because I trusted their judgment. It was easy to submit to my elders because I knew they had a certain level of wisdom that I was still working to acquire. It was not easy to submit to my lover because, frankly put, I feared what he would do if I gave him an authoritative position in my life.

I have been described by friends as being courageous, and I learned a long time ago that your approach determines your outcome. I decided to take a bold step, in to a position of submissiveness, in my relationships. I am not referring to the use of submission to postpone or avoid crucial conversations. I learned that being submissive is a behavior you display, not a banner you wave. It didn't always feel good, some people are only concerned about their own needs, even at the expense of someone else. But I learned through each situation. You'd be surprised how much you can see into someone when you approach him or her with a white flag in the air, arms down, in full surrender. I was able to judge character effortlessly in watching how a man, who I had been dating, responded to receiving full power. It is an indicator of whether someone believes in mutual respect or if they want to control your movements. I tried it out during arguments. I tried it when asked about the simple things like where we should go out to eat. The result is contrary to what most would expect. You will discover you became more powerful.

The truth is that most people really are not prepared to deal with someone in submissive mode. They expect fights. They expect conflict. They realize that they have their own fears and mistrusts. Being submissive has shifted the dynamics of relationships, in many cases softening my partner's actions toward me. An indicator of finding a good partner is when their reaction is to find a way to compromise and honor both of our needs when facing a problem. If we tried something completely their way and we failed, they came back to the table, acknowledged their misjudgment, and pursued my opinion on where we should go from here. Staying put and not aggressing created an opportunity for me to be pursued! It also allowed my partner to feel valued and to begin practicing submission toward me as well.

Submissiveness is greatly misunderstood and gets a bad wrap. Your submission doesn't mean you will be a doormat. It doesn't mean you don't have a mind. It's a quality of mind, a quality of psyche and behavior which is different than aggressive and dominating behavior. Men and women are naturally capable of both behaviors. Submission is often embraced by people who consider themselves assertive. The key concern is moving to solution and away from aggression.

Men don't want women that are masculinized and aggressive. This isn't a push against your independence, but if you appear to have it all under control, why would you need someone else? It's confusing to a man's natural instinct and behavior and they tend to move away to a path of less resistance. Both people can't be the dominant force; it's like two repelling magnets. You're power is not in between your legs, and what's *tweenst'* your legs doesn't define your femininity. Women shouldn't underestimate the power of their submission.

It's all about integrating it into your personality. I'm not always submissive in my relationships or social interactions, and I don't aspire to be. I have learned how to bring out the submissive woman inside me and use her when I want to gain insight about a date, friend, people I work with and family members. It is the first tool I use to attempt to resolve a conflict or situation.

I embrace that I am a strong, assertive, intelligent woman. I admire those parts of me and I will teach my *bonus* daughters and other young women how to possess those characteristics. However, I have also seen the power and positivity in submission, and learning to be submissive is an important lesson for any human being regardless of gender. I have communicated this to my sons as well.

All day long, men and women toil in the work force - a place of heady, logistical and competitive behavior - to find success. Much of this behavior comes from the left side of the brain, which deals with decision making and taking action. After the work day is over, the right side of the brain, which is creative, compassionate, emotional and communal, is allowed to come out and play. Women have a bit of an advantage here, in that our brains have a much larger corpus callosum (basically, a bridge between the left and right side of the brain) that allows for an easier transition between both styles of functioning. Men's bridge is much smaller and, thus, they seek that opposing energy. Where can we find that completion and comfort to let down our guard to our right side of the brain? Women have an uncanny ability to access that right side, bringing connections and energy between their brain and their heart. This is a bridge that links compassion, presence, tenderness, and emotion. Most men are not wired with a direct connection; the bridge is smaller and takes more care and practice to strengthen the connection. They seek out a tour guide- someone who can navigate the path with a demeanor that is more of an attendant and less of an authoritarian.

Time is a valuable resource. Wouldn't you rather spend your energy seeking solutions rather than defending your perspective? Next time you have a disagreement, try to focus on why your mate thinks and feels what he does. You can try by responding, "I can see your perspective. Now, if this is a good time, let me share where I'm coming from so we can figure out a way to make this work." Instead of setting you up as enemies, this approach helps affirm everyone's feelings, which brings you closer and makes it easier to come up with relationship rules that work for both of you.

# CROCK POT & VEGGIE MEALS

### CROCK POT JAMBALAYA
Serves: 6

- 12 ounces boneless skinless chicken breasts
- 1/2 cup green peppers, chopped
- 1 medium onion, chopped
- 2 celery ribs, sliced
- 4 garlic cloves, minced
- 1 (14 ounce) can diced tomatoes
- 1/3 cup tomato paste
- 1 (10.5 ounce) can chicken broth
- 1 teaspoon parsley
- 1 teaspoon thyme
- 1 1/2 teaspoons basil
- 1/2 teaspoon oregano
- 1 teaspoon Tabasco sauce
- 1 teaspoon cayenne pepper
- 1/2 teaspoon sea salt
- 1 teaspoon of Old Bays seasoning if available
- 1 bay leaf
- 1 pound shrimp, shelled
- 3 cups cooked rice

Cut chicken into 1 inch pieces.

Put all ingredients (EXCEPT shrimp and rice) in crock pot. Cover; cook on low for 8 hours.

Add shrimp the last 25 minutes of cooking. Stir in rice before serving.

## Da YARD BEEF STEW w/ Coconut dumplins

Serves: 5

- 3 sprigs thyme/ 1tablespoon dried thyme
- 1/3 cup all-purpose flour
- 1/4 teaspoon ground allspice
- 2 tablespoons brown sugar
- Sea salt and freshly ground white pepper
- 2 pounds beef stew meat, cut into 11/2-inch cubes
- 1pound Yukon gold potatoes, peeled and quartered
- 3 medium carrots, sliced
- 11-inch piece ginger, peeled and finely chopped
- 1clove garlic, finely chopped
- 2 teaspoons Worcestershire sauce (or Bragg's liquid amino soy sauce)
- 110-ounce can fire roasted diced tomatoes
- 2 jalapeno peppers/ 1/2 habanero pepper seeded and chopped
- 4 scallions, sliced (optional)

## COCONUT DUMPLINGS

- 1/2 cup grated coconut
- 1 ½ cups flour
- pinch of sea salt
- 1/2 cup coconut milk

Strip the leaves from 1sprig thyme and chop; combine with the flour, allspice,1/2 teaspoon salt and

1/4 teaspoon white pepper in a large bowl. Add the beef and toss to coat. Put the potatoes, carrots, the remaining 2 thyme sprigs, the ginger and garlic in a 5-to-6-quart slow cooker. Add the beef, reserving any excess seasoned flour in the bowl. Whisk 1/2 cup water and the Worcestershire sauce into the reserved seasoned flour, then add to the slow cooker. Pour the tomatoes on top. Cover and cook on low 7 hours or on high 4 hours.

An hour before the stew is done, you can start making the coconut dumplings.

It is firm dough with the ingredients mentioned above. Set the ball of dough aside to rest for about 10 minutes before shaping them into spinners. Break *off* small pieces of the dough (about a tablespoon full), using your palms, roll into a skinny cigar shape. Try to keep them the same size so they cook evenly.

Add the scallions to the stew and season with salt. Divide among bowls and serve.

## TROUBLE STEW
Serves: 4

I learned this dish while living in Nigeria. I love to cook it while listening to Fela Kuti's song: "Trouble Sleep Yanga Wake Am". West Africans refer to trouble as palava, so I guess you could refer to this recipe as Palava Stew.

- 1 Cup of Organic Palm Oil (packed full of nutritional benefits-vitamin E & carotenes)
- 4 Yellow Onions, diced
- 4 Large Roma Tomatoes, blanched, peeled and mashed or 1 can fire roasted diced tomatoes
- ½ habanero pepper, seeded & diced
- Sea Salt to taste
- Freshly ground Black Pepper
- ½ teaspoon thyme
- ½ minced garlic
- ½ pound of Red Snapper staked (you can also use ½ pound grass fed beef, diced)
- ¾ cup of dried shrimp (I find this at African or Asian markets)
- 3 bunches of fresh spinach or kale chopped
- ½ cup pumpkin seed, ground in a coffee grinder

Heat the palm oil in a medium pan (note, Palm Oil heats quickly) and fry the onions & minced garlic until golden. Add the tomatoes and the habanero, and season with black pepper. Cook for 10 minutes on low heat, stirring often.

Season with sea salt and add the diced meat or fish steaks, stir in the dried shrimp. Simmer on very low heat for 10 to 15 minutes, or until the spinach is soft and cooked. Stir regularly, being careful not to break up the fish too much.

Add the pumpkin seeds and stir them into the sauce. Cook for another 10 to 15 minutes on low heat, or until the sauce is thick and green.

## CHICKEN TACO SOUP
Serves 8

- 1 red onion, chopped
- 1 (16 ounce) can red kidney beans
- 1 (15 ounce) can black beans
- 1 bag frozen sweet whole kernel *corn,*
- 1 (8 ounce) can tomato sauce
- 1 (12 fluid ounce) can or bottle beer
- 2 (10 ounce) cans diced tomatoes ,undrained
- 2 minced jalapeno peppers
- 3 Tablespoons taco seasoning
- 3 whole skinless, boneless chicken breasts

### *Taco seasoning*

- 1 tablespoon chili powder
- 1/4 teaspoon garlic powder
- 1/4 teaspoon onion powder
- 1/4 teaspoon crushed red pepper flakes
- 1/4 teaspoon dried oregano
- 1/2 teaspoon paprika
- ½ teaspoons ground cumin
- 1 teaspoon sea salt
- 1 teaspoon black pepper
- shredded Cheddar cheese (optional)
- crushed tortilla chips (optional)

Place the onion, chili beans, black beans, corn, peppers, tomato sauce, beer, and diced tomatoes in a slow cooker. Add taco seasoning, and stir to blend. Lay chicken breasts on top of the mixture, pressing down slightly until just covered by the other ingredients. Set slow cooker for low heat, cover, and cook for 5 hours.

Remove chicken breasts from the soup, and allow to cool long enough to be handled. Stir the shredded chicken back into the soup, and continue cooking for 2 hours. Serve topped with shredded Cheddar cheese, and crushed tortilla chips, if desired.

## CROCK POT SPINACH & RICOTTA LASAGNA w/ TOSSED GREENS

Serves: 6

- 3 cups baby spinach
- 1 tablespoons basil
- 1 cup ricotta cheese
- 3/4 cup grated Parmesan (3 ounces) or asiago parmesan shredded mix
- 3 cups marinara sauce
- 6 regular lasagna noodles (not no-boil)
- 1 1/2 cups grated mozzarella (6 ounces)
- 2 tablespoons olive oil
- 2 teaspoons red wine vinegar
- Sea salt and black pepper
- 1 small head romaine lettuce or mixed greens, cut into strips (about 8 cups)
- 1 cucumber, thinly sliced
- 1/2 small red onion, thinly sliced
- Cherry tomatoes

In a bowl, mix together the spinach, ricotta, and Y2 cup of the Parmesan. In a second bowl, mix together the marinara sauce and 1/2 cup water.

Spread% cup of the marinara mixture in the bottom of a 4- to 6-quart crock pot. Top with 2 noodles(breaking to fit),1/2 cup of the remaining marinara mixture, half the spinach mixture, and 1/2 cup of the mozzarella; repeat. Top with the remaining noodles, marinara mixture, mozzarella, and Parmesan.

Cover and cook on low until the noodles are tender, 3 1/2 to 4 hours.

In a large bowl, whisk together the oil, vinegar, 1/2 teaspoon salt, and 1/2 teaspoon pepper. Add the lettuce/mixed greens, cucumber, cherry tomato, and onion and toss to combine. Serve with the lasagna.

## CROCK POT SCALLOPED POTATOES
Serves: 4

- 3 tablespoons butter
- 1/4 cup all-purpose flour
- 1tsp. salt
- 1/8 tsp. pepper
- 1 ½ cups milk
- 1to 1 ½ cups shredded cheese
- 5 medium potatoes, thinly sliced

Peel & Slice potatoes and turn potatoes into a buttered slow cooker. Combine butter, flour, salt and pepper together in saucepan over medium low heat. Whisk in milk gradually until no lumps remain. Heat and stir until bubbly and thickened. Stir in cheese to melt. Put sliced potatoes in crackpot; pour cheese sauce over. Cover and cook on low 5 to 7 hours.

## DRUNKEN OVERit BAKED BEANS

Serves: 6

- 1 pound dried Great Northern Beans
- 1/2 cup of strong coffee
- 1teaspoon butter
- 1 large onion, chopped
- 2 cloves of garlic, minced
- 1jalapeno, chopped
- 1/2 cup apple cider vinegar
- 1/2 c tomato paste
- dark brown sugar
- 1/2 cup molasses
- organic vegetable broth
- 1/2 teaspoon cayenne pepper
- 2 teaspoon of dry mustard
- 1/2 teaspoon thyme
- 1teaspoon black pepper
- 2 teaspoon salt

Soak beans overnight in a plastic container covered with cold water and stored in fridge.

The next; day pre heat oven to 250 degrees, place large oven safe pot over med heat. In a small saucepan, combine coffee, cider vinegar, butter, molasses, dry mustard, garlic, salt, pepper, thyme, and dry mustard. Bring to a slow boil and gently simmer sauce for 5 minutes. Remove from heat and stir in brandy, add in chopped onion and jalapenos cook about 5 min until the onions are soft. Stir in tomato paste, brown sugar and molasses (spray measuring cup with cooking spray before the molasses to help get it out easily)

Drain the beans, keeping the liquid stored in a measuring cup add beans to pot add enough vegetable broth to bean liquid to total 4 cups and add to pot raise heat to high and allow to come to a boil add cayenne, stir and cover pot with lid place in the oven for 6-8 hours until the beans are soft or 4 to 6 hours in a crock pot.

# BLACK EYED PEA FRITTERS WITH SPICY SAUCE

*I loved having these snacks in Nigeria.

- 1 cup of dried black-eyed peas sorted and soaked overnight., drained & rinsed. (Use frozen rather than canned if you need shorter prep time)
- 1/2 medium red onion, diced
- 1/2 cup of raw peanuts
- 1 teaspoon of minced thyme (you can use organic dried or fresh)
- 1/4 teaspoon cayenne pepper
- 1 tablespoon apple cider vinegar
- 1/4 cup water (add up to additional 2 tablespoons extra)
- 1 teaspoon sea salt
- 1/2 cup finely chopped green bell pepper
- 1 tablespoon cornmeal
- 5 cups of coconut oil

# HOT PEPPER SAUCE

- 1/4 cup extra virgin olive oil
- 1 small red onion, diced
- 1/2 teaspoon of cumin
- 1/8 of teaspoon of cayenne pepper
- Pinch of sea salt
- 1 large clove of garlic minced
- 1 minced habanero pepper (scotch bonnet pepper)
- 1/4 cup tomato sauce
- 1/4 cup tomato paste
- 1/8 teaspoon black pepper
- 2 teaspoons of apple cider vinegar
- 1/4 cup water
- Squeeze of lemon

Warm oil in a saucepan over medium heat. Add the onion, cayenne, cumin a pinch of sea salt, saute until the onions are caramelized, about 7 minutes.

Stir in the garlic, habanera, tomato paste, vinegar, tomato sauce and water. Mix well, and simmer for about 6 minutes.

Put all of the ingredients into a food processor, add the black pepper, and puree until smooth. Season with additional salt to taste. Store in a tightly sealed jar.

*BEANS*

Remove the skins from the beans (add them to a bowl of water, and sift them between their hands & fish out the skins that float to the top). In a food processor, combine the beans, onion, peanuts, thyme, cayenne, vinegar, water & salt and grind until completely smooth. Transfer to a medium bowl and refrigerate for 1hour.

Preheat stove top to 220F or medium high heat. Take the batter out of the refrigerator, add the bell pepper and cornmeal and whisk with a spoon or silicone cake blade for 2 minutes. In a medium skillet warm coconut oil over medium high heat, add spoonfuls (about 6) of batter into the oil to fry. If using gas heat, adjust flame to fry until golden brown, about 2 minutes.

Transfer the fritters to a paper towel-lined plate and allow them to drain.

## ITAL ISLAND PATTIES
Yields: 24 patties

Filling:

- 2 ½ cups black-eyed peas, bag or frozen
- 1 cup olive oil
- 1 large yellow onion; minced
- 4 large cloves garlic; minced
- 2 large carrots; peeled and minced
- 1 large medium bell pepper; seeded and minced
- 2 Scotch bonnet or fresh Serrano peppers; seeded and minced
- 2 large sweet potatoes; peeled and diced
- ½ tablespoon fresh thyme (leaves only)
- Coconut Aminos, freshly ground black pepper
- 2 cups oatmeal (or gluten free bread crumbs)

Pastry:

- 3 cups all-purpose flour
- 1/2 cup self-rising flour
- 2 ½ teaspoons ground curry powder
- 1 teaspoon sea salt
- 1 ½ cups vegetable shortening; chilled and diced, chilled water as needed
- 1 egg white/2 tablespoons water

Place the black-eyed peas in a large pan. Add water to cover by 2 inches. Bring to a boil, decrease the heat, and simmer, covered, for 30 to 50 minutes, or until the beans are tender. Drain, reserving 2 cups of the cooking water.

While the beans are cooking, make the pastry. Sift together the flours, turmeric, and salt into a bowl. Rub in the vegetable shortening with your fingers until the mixture resembles coarse crumbs.

Using a blunt, stainless-steel knife or a flat spoon, mix in enough chilled water to gather the mixture into a soft, pliable dough. Do not over handle the pastry. Shape it quickly into a ball. Cover pastry in a clean plastic bag and leave it in a cool place or the refrigerator for 30 minutes.

To make the filling, heat the olive oil in a large, heavy-based pan on medium heat. Fry the onion and garlic for about 5 minutes, or until they are soft and golden. Add the carrots, bell pepper, chiles/habeneros, and continue frying gently for 10 to 15 minutes, or until all the vegetables have softened and are half cooked.

Add the black-eyed peas, the 2 cups reserved cooking water and the potatoes, season with sea salt and pepper, cover the pan, decrease the heat, and simmer on low for 20 minutes or until the potatoes are tender. Remove from the heat, stir in the bread crumbs/instant oatmeal and set aside to cool.

Preheat the oven to 375 F. To make the patties, divide the chilled pastry into small, manageable portions for rolling out. On a lightly floured working surface, roll out each portion to a thickness of ¼ inches. Using a medium-size cookie cutter or saucer, cut out 24 rounds.

Place 1 to 2 teaspoons of the cooled filling on the center of each round, and moisten the edge of each round with a little chilled water. Carefully fold over half of each pastry round to form a crescent-shaped patty. Crimp the edge with the prongs of a fork to make a decorative seal. Repeat this process until you've used all the pastry and filling. Lightly glaze w/ egg white, water mixture.

Lightly grease and flour a baking sheet and carefully arrange the patties about 1 inch apart on the sheet. Bake in the oven for 25 to 30 minutes, or until golden brown. Serve hot or cold.

### IT'S YOUR SEASONed RICE
Serves 4 to 6

- 2/3 cup Organic Red Palm Oil
- 2 cups long grain white rice
- 3 ¼ cups boiling water/vegetable stock
- Sea salt, freshly ground black pepper
- 1 pound (500 g) grass fed beef or(*gardein beefless tips*)
- 2 white or yellow onions diced
- 4 cloves garlic minced
- 6 to 7 small Roma tomatoes; blanched, peeled and diced
- ½ cup raisins
- ½ cup pine nuts

In a large, heavy-based pan, heat ½ cup of the palm oil. When hot, add the rice and stir for 4 to 5 minutes, or until the rice is red, but transparent. Pour in enough boiling water to cover the rice. Season with sea salt and pepper, cover and simmer on low heat for about 20 minutes, being careful not to overcook.

In a separate large pan, heat the remaining oil. Fry the beef or meat substitute, onions, garlic, Roma tomatoes, raisins, and pine nuts for about 10 minutes, stirring constantly. Season to taste.

Stir this mixture into the rice. You may need to add some water to help the rice soften. Cover and simmer on low heat for about 10 minutes, or until the rice and meat are cooked and the rice absorbs all the stock. Serve hot.

## VEGGIE HERB BAKE
Serves 4

- 3 eggs (vegan substitute ¾ cup canned pumpkin)
- ¼ bunch kale; very finely shredded
- 1 large carrot; peeled and grated
- 1 small red bell pepper; seeded and diced
- 1 small jalapeno
- 6 tablespoons minced fresh green onions
- 1 tablespoons minced fresh basil
- 1 tablespoon minced fresh thyme
- 4 tablespoons self-rising flour
- 1 teaspoon sea salt
- 1 teaspoon freshly ground black pepper
- ¾ cup grated Cheddar or Gouda cheese/vegan cheese
- 1 tablespoon minced fresh cilantro
- 1 tablespoon chopped fresh flat-leaf parsley
- 1 small metal mixing bowl

Preheat the oven to 375 F

Separate the egg whites from the yolks, and set the whites aside. Combine the egg yolks, and set the whites aside. Combine the egg yolks and the kale, carrot, bell pepper, jalapeno, chives, basil, thyme, flour, salt, and pepper in a large bowl. Mix well. Whisk the egg whites (I put metal bowl in freezer to help create stiffer peaks) in a separate bowl until stiff peaks form. Using a wooden spoon, stir 2 spoonful's of egg whites into the vegetable mixture, then fold the remaining whisked egg whites into the mixture, taking care to work from the sides of the bowl toward the center to maintain the lightness of the mixture.

Grease a large Bundt pan and carefully pour the mixture into it. Evenly scatter the grated cheese over the top. Bake for 35 to 40 minutes, or until the dish is cooked through the center and brown on the edges. Remove from the heat and let stand for 10 minutes. Cover the dish with a large, flat plate and turn it upside down. Fill the center with cilantro and parsley. Serve hot.

## SWEET POTATO LOAF:
Serves 4 to 6

- 4 sweet potatoes or jewel yams; peeled and grated
- 3 cups grated pumpkin
- 1 tablespoon peeled and grated fresh ginger
- 4 tablespoons butter; melted
- ½ cups flaked; dried coconut or freshly grated coconut
- 1 cup cold coconut water
- 1 ¼ cups superfine sugar
- 1 teaspoon organic vanilla extract
- 1 teaspoon freshly grated nutmeg
- 4 tablespoons golden raisins (optional)
- 4 tablespoons dark raisins (optional)

Preheat the oven to 350 F

In a large mixing bowl, combine all the ingredients in food processor or mix well. Grease 2 9-inch pie dishes and pour in the mixture. Smooth the tops. Bake for 1 hour, or until firm. Serve hot or cold.

## BLACK BEAN STEW
Serves 8

- 4 cups dried black beans or black-eyed peas
- 2 smoked turkey leg, split into 4 pieces
- 2 organic spicy chicken sausage, sliced
- 2 tablespoons organic unrefined coconut oil
- 2 large red onions; diced
- 3 cloves garlic; crushed

- 6 to 10 green onions
- 1 bunch flat-leaf parsley
- 2 red bell peppers; seeded and diced
- 4 or 5 large roma tomatoes; diced
- 1 bay leaf
- 1 bunch of bok choy (cut-4 quarters)
- freshly ground black pepper
- Chile powder; for seasoning

*Spicy Sauce:*

- 2 red onions; diced,
- 3 fresh red jalapeños, minced
- 1 teaspoon cider vinegar
- juice of 2 to 3 lemons
- Sea salt
- 2 green onions chopped
- ½ cup olive oil
- ¼ cup chopped fresh flat-leaf parsley

Soak the beans overnight in plenty of water.

In a large pot, cook the beans boiling for 10 minutes and simmering for 20 in plenty of water. Drain the meats and cover with water/broth again. Bring to a boil for 1 minute. Drain and set aside. When the beans have cooked for 20 minutes, add the smoked turkey and the sausages. Cook slowly, adding more water if necessary, and season with salt.

In a large pan, melt the coconut oil. Sauté the red onions and garlic until the onions are golden. Tie the green onions and parsley together with kitchen twine to form a bouquet. Add the bell peppers, tomatoes, bay leaf, bouquet and bok choy, and season with pepper and Chile powder.

Cook slowly on low heat for 20 minutes, then add 2 ladles of beans. Mash together well, transfer to the remaining cooked beans and meat. Stir everything together and continue cooking until the sauce thickens and the meats are tender and well cooked. Taste for seasoning.

To make the sauce, combine all the ingredients in a gravy-boat. Just before serving, add a ladleful of strained liquid from the stew.

Serve the bean stew and the cooked meats separately, with the sauce.

## NEW BOO SAFFRON RICE
Serves 6 to 8

Saffron is made from dried, thin stamens of the crocus flower. Harvesting saffron is extremely labor intensive. It has been regarded in past centuries in Northern Africa as a food that reflects a family's wealth.

- 6 tablespoons butter (I use Organic Valley Pasteur Butter)
- 2 Cups Jasmine or Basmati Rice
- 2 green bell peppers, seeded and diced
- 3 green onions, diced w/ green tips
- 1 teaspoon saffron threads
- 1 teaspoon of sea salt
- 6 cardamon pods
- 1 teaspoon cayenne pepper
- ½ cup raisins
- 4 cups of water

Melt the butter in a large, heavy-based pan on medium heat. Fry the rice, onion and bell peppers, stirring intermittently for 15 minutes, or until the rice crisps and starts to brown. Add the saffron, salt, cardamon pods, cayenne, and water (if you have a rice cooker, add ingredients). Stir well, turn heat up to high until rolling boil, then turn down heat and simmer on low heat covered tightly for 25 minutes, until all of the water is absorbed and the rice is soft and cooked. Fluff the rice with a fork and remove cardamom pods and add raisins.

## POWER PEPPERED CHILI
Serves 4

- 2 roasted red bell peppers (I roast on oven rack)
- 2 poblano chiles
- 4 teaspoons olive oil
- 3 cups chopped zucchini
- 1 1/2 cups chopped red onion
- 4 garlic cloves, minced
- 1 tablespoon chili powder
- 1 teaspoon ground cumin
- 1/2 teaspoon Spanish smoked paprika
- 1/2 cup water
- 1/3 cup uncooked quinoa, rinsed
- 1/4 teaspoon sea salt
- 1 (14.5-ounce)BPA-free can fire-roasted diced tomatoes with chipotles, undrained
- 1 (15-ounce) BPA- free can no-salt-added black beans, rinsed and drained
- 1 cup low-sodium vegetable juice

Preheat broiler.

Cut bell peppers and chilies in half lengthwise; discard seeds and membranes. Place halves, skin sides up, on a foil-lined baking sheet, and flatten with hand. Broil 10 minutes or until blackened. Place in a paper bag; fold to close tightly. Let stand 10 minutes. Peel and coarsely chop.

Heat a large Dutch oven (heavy cooking pot with a tight fitting lid) over medium-high heat. Add oil to pan; swirl to coat. Add zucchini, onion, and garlic; sauté 4 minutes. Stir in chili powder, cumin, and paprika; sauté for 30 seconds. Add roasted peppers and chilies, 1/2 cup water, and remaining ingredients; bring to a boil. Reduce heat to medium-low; cover and simmer for 20 minutes or until quinoa is tender.

# WHAT THE KALE SALAD
Serves: 4

- 2 medium bunches kale, no stems-finely chopped (8 cups chopped)
- 2 large garlic cloves, minced
- 1/4 cup fresh lemon juice (from 1 lemon)
- 3-4 tablespoons extra virgin olive oil,
- 1/4 teaspoon fine grain sea salt
- 1/4 teaspoon freshly ground black pepper
- 2 handfuls dried sweetened cranberries, for garnish

*PECAN PARMESAN:*

- 1 cup pecan halves, toasted (previously soaked)
- 1.5 tablespoons nutritional yeast (Red Star Vegetarian Support Formula)
- 1 tablespoon extra virgin olive oil
- 2 pinches fine grain sea salt

Preheat the oven to 300F. Spread the pecans onto a baking sheet and toast in the oven for 8-10 minutes until fragrant and lightly golden.

Remove the stems from the kale and discard (you can save for smoothies if you enjoy!). Finely chop the kale leaves into very small pieces.

Wash the kale and spin dry. Place dried kale into a large bowl.

For the dressing: In a mini food processor, throw in minced garlic. Now add the lemon, oil, salt, and pepper and process until combined. Adjust to taste, if desired. Pour the dressing onto the kale and mix it into the kale with salad tongs. Keep mixing for about 1 minute to ensure everything is coated.

For the pecan 'cheese' parm: Using mini processor, add the pecans into the processor and process until the pecans are the size of peas. Add in the nutritional yeast flakes, oil, and salt and process again until it's a coarse crumb. For best texture- don't over-process - you don't want it powdery.

Sprinkle the pecan Parmesan all over the salad. Toss on a handful or two of dried cranberries.

## STELLA'S GROOVE BACK SALAD
Serves: 4 small

Salad:

- 5 cups packed kale, stems removed and roughly torn
- 1 ripe mango, chopped
- 1/2 large banana, sliced
- 1/2 cup fresh pineapple, diced
- 1 tablespoon shredded dried coconut
- 1/4 cup chopped macadamia nuts
- For the dressing:
- 1 cup chopped fresh pineapple
- 1/4 cup fresh lime juice
- 3/4 cup coconut milk (I like Blue Diamond)
- 1/4 tsp kosher salt
- 1 tablespoon hemp seeds
- 1 tablespoon coconut oil, melted

In a blender, blend all dressing ingredients until smooth.

Meanwhile, prepare the kale and add about 2/3 of the dressing to the kale and massage it in with your fingers. While it marinates, chop the fruit.

Mix everything together, top with coconut and mac nuts, and serve.

## HE'S the MAC WITH CHEEZE
Serves: 6

Cheeze Sauce:

- 3/4 cup unsweetened, unflavored almond milk (or more as needed to thin out)
- 6 Tablespoons nutritional yeast (Bob's Red Mill makes one in natural

food section of most grocery stores)
- 1 tablespoons Earth Balance or other non-dairy buttery spread
- 1 tablespoons all-purpose flour (or other flour)
- 2 tablespoons shallots, peeled and chopped
- 1 cup red or yellow potatoes, peeled and chopped
- 1/4 cup carrots, peeled and chopped
- 1/3 cup onion, peeled and chopped
- ¼ cup raw cashews
- 1 teaspoon Dijon mustard
- 1 tablespoon lemon juice, freshly squeezed
- 1/4 teaspoon black pepper
- 1/8 teaspoon cayenne

Mac:

- 4 quarts water
- 1 tablespoon sea salt
- 8 ounces macaroni
- 4 slices of bread, torn into large pieces
- 2 teaspoons sea salt
- 1/4 teaspoon garlic, minced
- 1/4 teaspoon paprika

In a large pot, bring the water and salt to a boil. Add macaroni and cook until al dente. In a colander, drain pasta and rinse with cold water. Set aside.

In a food processor, make breadcrumbs by pulverizing the bread and 1-2 tablespoons 'butter spread' to a medium-fine texture. Set aside.

Preheat oven to 350 degrees. In a saucepan, add shallots, potatoes, carrots, onion, and water, and bring to a boil. Cover the pan and simmer for 15 minutes, or until vegetables are very soft & drain, leaving ½ water.

In a blender, process the cashews, salt, garlic, 1/3 cup 'butter spread', mustard, lemon juice, black pepper, and cayenne. Add softened vegetables and cooking water to the blender and process until perfectly smooth.

In a large bowl, toss the cooked pasta and blended cheeze sauce until completely coated. Spread mixture into a 9 x 12 casserole dish, sprinkle with prepared breadcrumbs, and dust with paprika. Bake for 30 minutes or until the cheeze sauce is bubbling and the top has turned golden brown.

## TEX MEX ZUCCHINI w/ BLACK BEAN GUACAMOLE

- 2 medium zucchini, washed
- 1 tsp olive oil
- 1 clove of garlic, peeled + finely minced
- ¼ teaspoon ground chili pepper
- ¼ teaspoon ground oregano
- Sea salt & black pepper to taste

Hold the grater like a mandolin.

You put it on its side, with the face you want to use (the thickest grater) facing up, and use it just like you would a mandolin (minus the pain!!) moving the zucchini along it in long strokes to create the ribbons.

### *BLACK BEAN GUACAMOLE*:

- 2 avocados, pitted and flesh scooped out
- 1/2 cup diced red onion
- 1 small tomato, seeded and diced
- 1 (15-ounce) can black beans, drained and rinsed (about 1.5 cups cooked beans)
- 1/4 cup chopped cilantro leaves
- 2 tablespoons fresh lime juice, or to taste
- fine grain sea salt, to taste
- freshly ground black pepper, to taste
- red pepper flakes, to taste

Heat a skillet with the olive oil, then gently fry the zucchini with the garlic, chili pepper until slightly tender.

Brush some olive oil onto the zucchini and sprinkle with salt and pepper. When the zucchini is tender and you can easily separate the strands with a fork, it's ready. I like to check the zucchini after 5 minutes to make sure I'm not over cooking it. Be sure not to cook for too long or it will turn mushy.

While the zucchini is sautéing, prepare the black bean guacamole. Mash the avocado flesh in a large bowl. Fold in the onion, tomato, drained and rinsed black beans, and cilantro. Season to taste with lime juice, salt, pepper, and red pepper flakes.

Remove zucchini from the pan, flip over. Now sprinkle on some chili powder, cumin, oregano, salt, and pepper (as much or as little as you want). Top the zucchini with guacamole and serve warm.

Pile it into a dish (I served mine on a bed of raw spinach leaves), and grate over and organic cheddar cheese or cheese substitute.

### SAUTEED BEANS and ZUCCHINI
Serves: 4 to 6

- 2 cups filtered water
- ¼ pound fresh string beans, stemmed and halved
- ¼ pound yellow string beans, stemmed and halved
- 4 tablespoons olive oil
- 1 small onion, sliced
- ¼ teaspoon curry powder
- 1 medium organic green zucchini, chopped
- 1 medium sweet red pepper, chopped
- 1 small tomato, cut into wedges
- ½ teaspoon sea salt
- ¼ teaspoon black pepper
- 1 sprig fresh thyme

In a medium saucepan, bring water to boil. Add beans and cook for 4 minutes. Drain beans and set aside. In a medium saucepan, over medium heat, sauté beans, onions and curry powder in oil for 2 minutes.

Add remaining ingredients and sauté for another 3-5 minutes. Remove thyme before serving.

## KALE FRITTERS
Serves: 4 to 6

- 2 cups of fresh kale, chopped
- 1 small red onion, diced
- 1 small tomato, chopped
- 1 tablespoon coconut oil, melted
- ½ cup filtered water
- 1 large egg beaten, (see vegan substitute below-make first)
- 1 ½ cups flour (or gluten free substitute)
- 1 tablespoon baking powder
- ¼ teaspoon sea salt
- ¼ teaspoon black pepper
- ½ cup vegetable oil/coconut oil

Try the flax egg: 1 tablespoon of ground flaxseed meal mixed with 3 tablespoon of water (or hemp milk, wine or beer) and then let it sit for 10 minutes or until it gelatinous, like an egg. (You will probably need to double this or add more liquid if you're frying a big batch of something). If you don't have ground flaxseed meal, you can try subbing 1 tablespoon of cornstarch instead.

If the food you're about to fry simply needs to be moistened so the flour sticks to it, try dipping it in soda water or beer.

In a large saucepan over low heat, combine kale, onion, tomato, melted coconut oil, and water. Cover and steam for 10 minutes. Set aside and cool, then add beaten egg or flax egg substitute.

In a large bowl, combine flour, baking powder, salt and pepper. Stir in kale mixture to form a batter, adding water if the batter is too stiff. In a large, heavy saucepan or deep fryer, heat oil to 360F. Drop tablespoons of batter; 5 at a time, into oil and deep-fry until golden.

## CHICK PEA PANCAKES & CURRY RUN DOWN (T)
Serves: 2 medium pancakes

To prevent it from sticking to the skillet, be sure to spray the skillet liberally with olive oil before pouring on the batter. Also, I suggest chopping the veggies finely so they cook faster.

- 1 green onion, finely chopped (about 1/4 cup)
- 1/4 cup finely chopped red pepper
- 1/2 cup chickpea flour (also known as garbanzo flour)
- 1/4 teaspoon garlic powder
- 1/4 teaspoon fine grain sea salt
- 1/8 teaspoon freshly ground black pepper
- 1/4 teaspoon baking powder
- pinch red pepper flakes
- 1/2 cup + 2 tablespoons water

Prepare the vegetables and set aside. Preheat a 10-inch skillet over medium heat.

In a small bowl, whisk together the chickpea flour, garlic powder, salt, pepper, baking powder, and optional red pepper flakes.

Add the water and whisk well until no clumps remain. I like to whisk it for a good 15 seconds to create lots of air bubbles in the batter.

Stir in the chopped vegetables.

When the skillet is pre-heated (a drop of water should sizzle on the pan), spray it liberally with olive oil or other non-stick cooking spray.

Pour on all of the batter (if making 1 large pancake) and quickly spread it out all over the pan. Cook for about 5-6 minutes on one side (timing will depend on how hot your pan is), until you can easily slide a pancake flipper/spatula under the pancake and it's firm enough not to break when flipping. Flip pancake carefully and cook for another 5 minutes, until lightly golden. Be sure to cook for enough time as this pancake takes much longer to cook compared to regular pancakes.

Serve on a large plate and top with your desired toppings (Curry veggies below). Leftovers can be wrapped up and placed in the fridge. Reheat on a skillet until warmed throughout.

## CURRY

- 2 medium potatoes
- 3 cups or 4 sweet potatoes
- 2 ½ cups pumpkin, de-seeded and peeled
- 1/2 cauliflower, chopped
- 1 red pepper, chopped
- ½ Habenero pepper or 3 jalapeno peppers, seeded & diced
- 2 cups green beans
- Coriander (pinch)
- 1 ½ cups or 1 BPA free can Coconut Milk
- 2 tsp Mild Curry Powder
- 3 tsp Ground Allspice
- 1 red onion, chopped
- 1 tsp Organic Dried Thyme
- 1 tsp minced garlic
- 1 spring onion, chopped
- 2 tablespoons vegetable oil

Cut all of the vegetables into bite-sized pieces.

Heat the oil in a large frying pan on a medium heat, then add the spring onion, thyme, onion, all spice, garlic and curry powder.

Keep stirring until the onions are lightly browned.

Stir in the premium coconut milk and mix well. Add a small amount of water if necessary (perhaps 1/3 cup). Add the potatoes and cook for 10 minutes (or until soft).

Lower the heat and add the remaining vegetables. Cover and simmer for another 10 minutes.

## BANANA BREAD POWA BARS
Yields: 10 Bars

Dry ingredients:

- 2/3 cup gluten-free rolled oats
- 1/2 cup raw buckwheat groats*, ground into flour (in bulk bins @ Whole Foods)
- 1/2 cup chopped walnuts
- 1/4 cup shredded unsweetened coconut
- 3 tablespoons chia seeds
- 3 tablespoon mini dark chocolate chips
- 1/4 tsp cinnamon
- ¼ tsp nutmeg
- 1/4 tsp fine grain sea salt

Wet ingredients:

- 3/4 cup mashed ripe banana (about 2 medium)
- 1/2 cup natural smooth peanut butter
- 1/4 cup coconut nectar syrup
- 1 tsp pure vanilla extract

Preheat oven to 350F and line an 8-inch square pan with 2 pieces of wax/parchment paper, one going each way. Note – to get the parchment to stick to the pan, give the base a spray with olive oil.

Add raw buckwheat groats into a high-speed processor and blend on high until a fine flour forms. Whisk all dry ingredients together in a mixing bowl.

Mash bananas until smooth and measure out 3/4 cup. Stir together the banana and all the wet ingredients in a bowl.

Add the wet mixture to the dry mixture and stir well until combined. The dough should be very sticky!

Scoop batter into prepared pan. Place a piece of parchment paper on top of the batter and press it down to spread out the batter evenly. Make sure it's as even as possible.

Bake at 350F for 22-26 minutes, or until the edges are golden brown and the bread is firm to touch. Cool in the pan completely (I left it for 1 hour) before removing and slicing into bars.

## HE'S FAKIN BACON

- 3 1/2 cups flaked coconut
- 2 tablespoons liquid smoke
- 1 tablespoon Coconut aminos or Braggs aminos
- 1 tablespoon pure maple syrup
- 1 tablespoon water
- 1 teaspoon smoked paprika (optional)

Preheat oven to 300 degrees.

Combine liquid smoke, Coconut aminos/ Braggs, maple syrup, and water in a large mixing bowl. Pour in flaked coconut, using a wooden spoon to gently toss the coconut in the liquid mixture. If adding smoked paprika, add and toss to coat evenly. Once the coconut is evenly coated, pour it onto a non-stick baking sheet (I spray mine lightly with coconut oil) and slide it the oven. Bake for 20 minutes, using a spatula to flip the 'bacon' about every 5 minutes so it cooks evenly. Be mindful, it WILL burn if you're not keeping an eye on it and regularly flipping it. Coconut bacon can be stored in a sealed bag or container for up to a month, refrigerator optional. Nice for BLTs or as salad topping.

## CRISPY TENDERONIES
**You will leave the chicken nuggets!**
Serves: 4

- 2 cups cauliflower florets (about 1/2 head of cauliflower)
- 1/4 cup high heat oil, for frying (coconut, and avocado oils are all great high-heat options)

*Flax 'Breading':*

- 1/4 cup ground flax
- 1/4 cup almond meal
- 3/4 cup water

*Flour Mix:*

- 1 ½ cups bread crumbs (gluten-free or regular)
- 1/4 cup almond meal
- 1 teaspoon organic cane sugar
- 2 tablespoons nutritional yeast
- 1/2 teaspoon garlic salt
- 1/2 teaspoon sea salt
- 1/4 teaspoon cracked black pepper
- 1/4 teaspoon cayenne pepper

In a small bowl, make flax wash by mixing ground flax, almond meal, and water. Set aside. Next, mix together in a medium-sized mixing bowl the bread crumbs, almond meal, sugar, nutritional yeast, garlic salt, salt, pepper, and cayenne. This mixture will become your breading.

Heat 1/4 cup oil n a large frying pan over medium heat. Dip cauliflower florets into the flax wash mixture, coating lightly but evenly. Next, dip cauliflower into the flour mixture and coat completely. Drop coated cauliflower nuggets into the heated oil, and cook until golden and crunchy, then flip and repeat until the nugget is evenly fried, about 2-3 minutes on each side.

Using tongs, move cooked nuggets to a paper towel lined plate to absorb excess oil, let cool several minutes, then enjoy with you're the below dipping sauce! They are best if eaten immediately. Uneaten nuggets can be reheated in the oven at 375 degrees for 10 minutes, or until warm.

**Staying away from fried foods? You can try baking these at 400 degrees for about 20-30 minutes, flipping halfway through. Not nearly as crunchy and crispy, but probably much healthier.

*For the Mango Dipping Sauce:*

- 1 cup frozen mango chunks, thawed
- 1 cup mayonnaise
- ¼ cup fresh cilantro leaves
- 2 tablespoons honey
- 1 teaspoon lemon juice
- 6 to 8 drops Hot n Saucy (add more if you like it a bit more spicy)

## Hot n Saucy
Yields: 2 pints

- 1 teaspoon vegetable oil
- 18 fresh Scotch Bonnet peppers, sliced and seeded
- 6 fresh jalapeno peppers, sliced
- 6 cloves garlic, crushed
- 1/2 cup minced onion
- 3/4 teaspoon sea salt
- 2 cups water
- 1/4 cup distilled white vinegar
- 3 tablespoons raw honey/ 2 tablespoons coconut sugar

In a large sauce pan over medium-high heat, combine oil, peppers, garlic, onion, and salt; cook for 5 minutes, stirring frequently.

Pour in water, and cook for 20 minutes, or until the ingredients are soft. Stir frequently. Remove from heat, and allow mixture to cool to room temperature.

Transfer the mixture to a blender, and puree until smooth. Pour in vinegar and honey/coconut sugar; blend until mixed. Keep refrigerated.

## SHAKIN THAT BUDDHA BOWL
Serves: 3

*For roasting and serving:*

- 1 head broccoli, chopped into bite-sized pieces
- 1 head cauliflower, chopped into bite-sized pieces
- 1.5 cups cooked chickpeas, drained and rinsed (or one 15-oz can)
- 1 Tablespoon Olive Oil, divided
- Pinch cayenne pepper
- Salt & Pepper
- Cooked grains, for serving (optional)

*For the dressing:* (can stay 5 days in refrigerated container)

- ½ cup cashews, soaked
- 2 tablespoons fresh lemon juice
- 1 tablespoons tahini (ground hulled sesame seed from North Africa)
- 1 large garlic clove, chopped
- ¼ tsp fine grain sea salt
- ¼ cup nutritional yeast
- 6 tablespoons water, or as needed to thin out

Pour boiling water over cashews and let sit in the bowl for at least 45 minutes. Preheat oven to 400F and line two large baking sheets with parchment paper.

Place chopped broccoli and cauliflower onto one baking sheet. Drizzle with 2 tsp oil and mix with hands until coated. Sprinkle with salt and pepper. Set aside.

Place a couple paper towels on the other baking sheet and spread out the drained and rinsed chickpeas.

Place 2 more paper towels on top and roll the chickpeas around until completely dry. Drizzle with 1 tsp olive oil and roll around the chickpeas with your hands until they are all coated. Sprinkle with sea salt, cayenne and black pepper.

Roast the broccoli, cauliflower and chickpeas for 15 minutes at 400F. After 15 minutes, give the chickpea pan a gentle shake to roll them around in the pan. Roast both pans for another 10-15 minutes or until the broccoli and cauliflower are cooked through and the chickpeas are golden in color.

Meanwhile, prepare the dressing by adding all dressing ingredients into a blender and blending on high speed until smooth.

When the vegetables and chickpeas are ready, remove from oven and place into a large mixing bowl. Add your desired amount of dressing on top and toss until coated. Season to taste. Serve over a warm bed of grains with more dressing drizzled on top.

## SPICY Q'd CORN ON THE COB

- 6 ears of local corn
- 2 tablespoons lime juice
- 2 tablespoons organic unrefined coconut oil
- ½ teaspoon cayenne pepper
- ½ teaspoon sea salt
- ½ teaspoon black pepper
- Dash of paprika

Peel leaves from corn, leaving at least 6 leaves on the cob. Pull these leaves back to expose corn. Set aside.

Preheat grill to 300F

In a bowl, combine lime juice, oil, and spices. With a pastry brush, bush mixture on corn. Pull leaves over cobs. Then grill until corn is cooked, about 15 minutes. Remove charred husks before serving.

## SHE-RA CHIA BREAD

Packed with 7 grams of fiber and 9 grams of protein.

- 1/2 cup hemp/chia seeds (I prefer walnut like taste of hemp seeds)
- 1/2 cup raw sunflower seeds
- 1/2 cup raw pumpkin seeds
- 1/2 cup gluten-free rolled oats, ground into a flour
- 1/4 cup quinoa flour (or more oat flour)
- 1 teaspoon dried oregano
- 1 teaspoon coconut sugar/ organic cane sugar
- 1/2 teaspoon dried thyme
- 1/2 teaspoon fine grain sea salt
- 1/4 teaspoon garlic powder
- 1/4 teaspoon onion powder
- 1 cup water

Preheat oven to 325F and line a 9-inch square pan with two pieces of parchment paper, covering bottom.

Add rolled oats and buckwheat into a high-speed blender. Blend on highest speed until a fine flour forms.

Add all dry ingredients into a large bowl and stir well until combined. Stir in the water until combined.

The mixture will be very watery and runny at first, but it will thicken up fairly quick. Scoop it into the pan and spread it out with a spatula as evenly as possible. You can use lightly wet hands to smooth it down if necessary. Sprinkle the bread with fine grain sea salt before going into the oven.

Bake at 325F for about 20 minutes, or until firm to the touch. Let cool in the pan for 5 minutes and then lift it out and transfer it to a cooling rack for another 5-10 minutes. Slice and enjoy!

This bread keeps for 2-3 days only, past that will make it gummy in texture. You can freeze for enduring freshness, toast it straight from the freezer

## TURNIN HEADS SNACK BREAD
Serves: 4 to 6

- 3 cups flour (3 cups almond flour)
- 2 tablespoons baking powder
- ½ teaspoon sea salt
- ½ teaspoon nutmeg
- ½ teaspoon ground allspice
- 1 cup organic brown sugar
- 1 cup lukewarm filtered water
- 3 tablespoons organic unrefined coconut oil
- 2 tablespoons molasses
- Flour for dusting

Preheat oven to 375F. In a large bowl, sift together the flour, baking powder, sea salt, nutmeg, and allspice. Dissolve the sugar in water.

Combine with melted coconut oil and molasses and add to flour mixture to form firm dough. Vigorously knead dough to smoothen. On a lightly floured metal bowl (turn bowl over), place ball (golf ball sized) of dough on top of bowl and push dough around round bottom of bowl. Lightly dust with flour. Bake on greased baking sheet for about 30 minutes. Serve warm or at room temperature.

# FRIED GUACAMOLE

- 1 ripe avocado
- juice of 1 medium lime
- 3 to 4 tablespoons diced scallions (the white part is great) or diced red onion
- 3 cloves of minced garlic
- 2 tablespoons finely diced jalapeno (deseeded to remove some of the spice)
- a bit of chopped cilantro
- sea salt and coarse ground black pepper to taste
- wonton wrappers
- 1 egg, beaten (optional) melted butter/corn starch w/water mix
- thin scallion green strips
- canola oil for frying

Mash avocado in a small bowl. Stir in lime juice, scallions or onions, jalapeno, cilantro, garlic, and salt and pepper. Mash well so that the avocado is relatively smooth. Set aside.

On a clean work surface, set out six wanton wrappers. Brush lightly with beaten egg (optional). Dollop about 1 teaspoon of avocado mixture into the center of the wanton. Roll into a small pouch, pinching the wanton skin around each side of the avocado mixture. The egg will help seal the pinched ends. Very gently tie a scallion green on each end of the wanton. Repeat until all six avocado packages are done. Then repeat until all of the avocado mixture is done. Assembled pouches can be frozen on a single layer until frozen through. They can be carefully-stacked in a freezer-safe container. When ready to fry, remove pouches from the freezer, place in a single layer on a plate, allow to defrost for about 30 minutes then fry according to the instructions below.

To fry pouches, place oil in a shallow, heavy bottom sauté pan. The oil should be about 1-inches deep. Heat over medium heat. To test the oil, dip a corner of a wanton skin in the oil. If it begins to strongly sizzle, you're ready to go. Place three avocado stuffed wantons into the hot oil. Cook for about

45 seconds on each side, using a pair of tongs to rotate. The wantons may need a bit longer if they've been frozen. Remove when wanton is golden brown and crispy on all sides. Allow to rest on a few sheets of paper towels

## CABBAGE & CORN
Serves 3-4

- 1bag frozen sweet corn
- 2 cups shredded cabbage
- 1medium onion diced
- 1tbsp oil
- 1medium tomato (chopped)
- 2 tablespoon water
- 1scotch bonnet pepper diced and de-seeded (optional)
- A dash of black pepper (optional)

Wash the cabbage then shred it. Saute the onion (stir so it does not stick)

Add the shredded cabbage, tomatoes, black pepper water and stir. Cover saucepan and cook cabbage for about 7 minutes until tender. Add de-seeded scotch bonnet pepper (optional) Add the frozen corn.

Simmer for another 3-4 minutes

Serve with any of these items: rice, boiled green banana, fried dumplings.

## QUINOA CHICK BURGERS
Yields: 4

- 1 small sweet potato - 1/2 cup mashed
- 1 cup chick peas (I use thawed frozen)
- 1/2 cup quinoa (cooked according to directions)
- 4 scallions, minced
- 2 garlic cloves/ 1 teaspoon minced
- 1 teaspoon allspice
- medium red onion, thinly diced
- 1 teaspoon cumin
- 1/2 teaspoon saffron
- 1 teaspoon curry powder
- dash ginger powder
- 1 tbsp oil
- 2 tsp coconut milk powder
- 2 tsp arrowroot powder
- 1 teaspoon thyme
- Pinch sea salt and 1/2 lime squeezed- optional
- 4 tablespoon corn flour (+some for dusting)
- water

Bake sweet potato and cook the quinoa adding the curry, cumin and saffron on the stove top, whisking with fork until fluffy.

Blend the fresh seasoning with the chick peas, add some lime juice/water and the oil to make it moist. Mash together with sweet potato. Add the coconut powder, arrowroot powder, cumin, saffron to flavor.

Combine the quinoa with the sweet potato, chick pea mixture and add 4 large tablespoons of corn flour. Use palms to mold into burgers/patties, and dust with corn flour. Set on lightly oiled cookie sheet and bake at 325F for 15 minutes or until golden brown on each side.

## BAKED SWEET POTATO FRIES
Serves: 4

- 4 medium shaped sweet potatoes (about 2 pounds), peeled
- 1 teaspoon sea salt
- 1 teaspoon of black pepper
- 1/2 teaspoon of cayenne pepper
- 1 teaspoon of paprika
- 1 tablespoon extra- virgin olive oil

Cut the potatoes into 1/2-inch thick slices, and then cut them length-wise into the shape of a fry. Preheat oven to 450F

Wash & Drain in a colander and pat well with a paper towel to dry- if they aren't dry the olive oil won't stick.

In a large bowl, Mix all other ingredients together in a large bowl and toss with the potatoes until they are evenly coated.

Transfer the potatoes to a large baking sheet covered with parchment paper. Spread the potatoes in a single layer. Try not to overcrowd or have multiple layers of fries- you want them to be roasted, not steamed.

Place in the oven and cook for 30-35 minutes, turning the fries once or twice during that time to cook evenly. May take more or less time, depending on the size and thickness you cut the fries.

Remove once the edges slightly begin to brown and fries begin to crisp. Sprinkle sea salt on top when they are hot out of the oven.

# MOODY CHICKS PEAS

Serves: 8

- 1 tablespoons coconut oil
- 1 tablespoon red palm oil
- 2 onions, minced
- 2 cloves garlic, minced
- 2 teaspoons fresh ginger root, finely chopped
- 6 whole cloves/ 1/2 teaspoon allspice
- 2 (2 inch) sticks cinnamon, crushed
- 1 teaspoon ground cumin
- 1 teaspoon ground coriander
- Sea salt
- 1 teaspoon cayenne pepper
- 1 teaspoon ground turmeric
- 2 (15 ounce) cans garbanzo beans (BPA-free can)
- 1 cup chopped fresh cilantro

Heat oils in a large frying pan over medium heat, and fry onions until tender.

Stir in garlic, ginger, cloves/allspice, cinnamon, cumin, coriander, salt, cayenne, and turmeric. Cook for 1 minute over medium heat, stirring constantly. Mix in garbanzo beans and their liquid. Continue to cook and stir until all ingredients are well blended and heated through. Remove from heat. Stir in cilantro just before serving, reserving 1 tablespoon to sprinkle on top.

# CAPPACINO MUFFINS (C)

Serves: 12 muffins

- 2 cups all-purpose flour
- 1/2 cup sugar
- 2-1/2 teaspoons baking powder
- 2 teaspoons instant espresso coffee powder (or instant coffee)
- 1/2 teaspoon salt
- 1/2 teaspoon cinnamon
- 1/4 teaspoon nutmeg
- 1 cup whole milk
- 1/2 cup butter, melted and cooled
- 1 egg, slightly beaten
- 1 teaspoon vanilla extract
- 3/4 cup semi-sweet chocolate mini-chips

Preheat oven to 375 degrees F. Line muffin tins with papers or grease liberally.

In a large bowl, whisk together flour, sugar, baking powder, espresso or instant *coffee*, salt, cinnamon, and nutmeg. Set aside.

In a medium bowl, mix milk, butter, egg, and vanilla until combined. Stir milk mixture into flour mixture only until combined. It's important you don't over mix. Fold in chocolate chips.

Fill muffin cups 3/4 full. Bake 15 to 20 minutes for standard muffins, 10 to 12 minutes for mini-muffins. These muffins freeze well.

## PASSION PORRIDGE

Serves: 3

- 1/2 Cup water
- 2 cups of almond/coconut milk
- 1 cinnamon stick
- 1/2 cup of quinoa
- 1/2 cup amaranth
- 1 teaspoon of sea salt
- 1/2 teaspoon of coconut oil
- 1 cup dried banana chips
- 1/2 cup raisins
- 1 tablespoon flaxseed/chia powder
- 2 teaspoons of agave nectar

Bring a saucepan over medium-high heat and combine; water, Almond/Coconut Milk, cinnamon stick, quinoa, amaranth, salt and coconut oil. Bring to a boil, while continually stirring; quickly reduce the heat to low. Cover and simmer for 20 minutes.

Add the raisins, banana chips, flaxseed/chia powder, and agave nectar, and stir into the quinoa mixture. Add more milk if needed. Remove from heat, let stand for 5 minutes, then serve.

# PLANTAIN POWER PORRIDGE
Serves: 4

- 5 to 6 Plantain
- 2 cups Coconut / Almond Milk
- 1cup Water
- 1tsp Cinnamon or 1large Cinnamon Stick
- 1/2 teaspoon Nutmeg
- 1/4 teaspoon Allspice
- 1teaspoon Sea Salt or to taste
- 1teaspoon Vanilla extract
- 1cup Sweetened Condensed Milk or agave to taste

Cut ends off plantain, make an incision along the side and using thumbs, peel the skin form the plantains, cut in 3 or 4 pieces each and place in a bowl of water mixed with 1tsp of lemon juice, which will prevent them from turning brown

Combine 1cup of coconut/almond milk with 1cup of water

Blend the plantain with the milk/water liquid, adding one piece of plantain at a time.

Pour the banana mixture into a pot on Medium-High heat. Using a non-stick pot will save clean up time later.

Stir in cinnamon, nutmeg, allspice and salt and continue stirring until blended.

Continue stirring on Low heat until the porridge thickens, about 15 minutes. If needed, heat remaining

1cup of milk and add slowly to pot until you reach your desired consistency.

Add vanilla, and sweeten with sweetened condensed milk to taste.

## BREAKFAST BANANA FRITTERS
Serves: 12 fritters

- 1 1/2 cup mashed overripe Bananas  ( 5 medium bananas)
- 3 Tablespoons Brown Sugar
- 1/2 teaspoon Nutmeg
- 1/2 teaspoon Cinnamon
- 1 teaspoon Vanilla extract
- pinch Sea Salt
- 1cup all-purpose Flour
- 1-2 tablespoon Cooking Oil  (Coconut Oil)
- 1Tablespoon raw cane Sugar

Mash bananas with sugar and spices; stir flour into banana mixture.

Heat 1to 2 Tbsp cooking oil on High *and*, using a serving spoon, spoon batter into pan.

Fry fritters until crisp and brown on both sides; you may have to add more cooking oil. Press on them with a spatula, if no batter oozes out they're done.

Remove fritters from pan and place on paper towel. Sprinkle with cane sugar and eat warm.

## WILD N OUT SALAD
Serves: 4 to 6

- 1cup wild rice -make sure it is rinsed & soaked overnight (I prefer Royal Blend, Rice Select-omits soaking)
- 1/2 teaspoon sea salt
- 1green bell pepper, seeded and diced
- 1red bell pepper, seeded and diced
- 1orange bell pepper, seeded and diced
- 2 large stalks of bok choy, rinsed & sliced

- 1/2 cup thinly sliced scallions (green onions)
- 1/2 cup raisins
- 1/2 cup toasted almonds

Cook wild rice according to directions or in a medium saucepan turn heat to high, combine the rice with 3 cups of water & bring to a boil. Add the salt, reduce heat to low & cover, simmer for 30 minutes.

Remove from heat, transfer to a strainer and rinse under cold water for a few minutes, or until rice is room temp.

In a large bowl, combine the cooked wild rice, peppers, raisins, scallions and almonds- toss.

Refrigerate for 1hour to allow flavors to seep.

## PLANTAIN DRESSING

- 1ripe plantain (skin should be black)
- half a red onion, minced
- 1/2 teaspoon allspice/ 1pimento
- 2 scallions
- ginger powder or a piece of ginger
- dash Braggs liquid amino (soy sauce) / 1teaspoon sea salt
- 1tsp olive oil (you could try another like sesame, almond or coconut)

Add all ingredients to a blender or food processor, puree until creamy.

## GINGER PEANUT DIPPING SAUCE
Serves: 4

- 1large tablespoon minced ginger
- 1/2 cup roasted peanuts
- 1/2 cup apple juice
- 1large teaspoon agave nectar
- 1/8 teaspoon of cayenne pepper
- 1 teaspoon sea salt

In a blender or food processor, combine the ginger, peanuts, apple juice, agave nectar, cayenne and salt and blend until creamy. Transfer to a serving bowl, or double portions and store in jar in the refrigerator. Great for sweet potato fries!!

## CHILL OUT SWEET TANGY BROCCOLI SALAD
Serves: 4-6

- 2 ½ teaspoons sea salt
- 2 large heads of broccoli, florets separated, stalks peeled & sliced thin
- 2 tablespoons of orange juice/mango juice
- 1 tablespoon of fresh squeezed lime juice
- 2 tablespoons fresh squeezed lemon juice
- 1 tablespoon of agave
- 1 teaspoon fresh basil, minced
- 9 tablespoons of extra-virgin olive oil
- 3 cloves minced garlic

In a large pot over high heat, bring 3 quarts of water to a boil, add 2 teaspoons of salt, and wait until it dissolves. Remove pot from heat, add the broccoli for one minute until the color is bright green, then drain.

In a blender, make the marinade by mixing the orange/mango juice, lime juice, lemon juice, agave, basil, garlic and ½ teaspoon of salt. Blend while slowly adding the olive oil.

Place the broccoli in a large bowl and toss with marinade. Cover and chill for at least 30 minutes. Serve chilled.

## BLUEBERRY LIME SALSA
Serves: 1 1/2 cups

- 1 cup fresh blueberries
- 5 medium strawberries
- 1/4 red onion
- 1 teaspoon lime zest

- juice of two limes
- 1/3 cup fresh cilantro leaves
- ½ avocado, chopped
- salt and pepper to taste

Combine blueberries, strawberries, onion, lime zest, juice and cilantro in a food processor or blender and set to pulse. Make to the consistency you like, I like to leave mine a bit chunky, so I only pulse it.

about 5-6 times. Taste and season with salt and pepper if desired. Scrape salsa into a bowl and fold in chopped avocado. Serve with tortilla or pita chips, or on top of fish or chicken.

## CORNMEAL & CURRANT PUDDING
Serves: 4

- 2 cups cornmeal
- 2 cups sweet yams , grated
- 1 cup flour (gluten free:1/3 cup tapioca starch/flour & 2/3 cup brown rice flour)
- ¼ cup carrots, grated
- 1 ½ cups coconut milk
- 1 ½ cup organic raw cane sugar
- 1 tablespoon organic vanilla extract
- 2 tablespoon grass-fed organic butter (unrefined organic coconut oil)
- 1 teaspoon ground nutmeg
- ½ teaspoon ground cinnamon
- ½ cup dried currants/raisins

Preheat oven to 350F

In a medium bowl, combine cornmeal, yams, flours, and carrots. In a separate bowl, mix the coconut milk with the sugar, vanilla extract, and melted butter/coconut oil. Stir well.

Mix in cornmeal mixture, nutmeg, salt, and currants. Pour into a 10" round baking pan and bake for 1 to 1 ¼ hours until pudding is a bit soft, but firm when shaken.

## SWEET TATO PUDDIN'
Serves: 4

- 2 lbs sweet potatoes, grated
- ¼ lb yellow yams, grated (I buy from African store)
- ½ cup flour
- ¼ cup cornmeal
- ½ cup raisins
- 4 cups coconut milk
- 1 cup organic cane brown sugar
- 1 teaspoon nutmeg
- ½ teaspoon sea salt
- 2 tablespoons white rum
- ¼ cup melted butter (organic unrefined coconut milk)

Preheat oven to 350F

In a large bowl, mix together sweet potatoes, yams, flour, cornmeal, and raisins. Set aside. In a medium bowl, combine coconut milk and brown sugar. Add nutmeg, salt, organic vanilla extract, rum, and melted butter/coconut oil.

Pour into potato mixture. Beat until smooth.

Pour batter into a greased 9" baking pan.

Allow to rest for 10 minutes, then bake for 1 to 1 ¼ hours until pudding is a bit soft, but firm when shaken.

# 'MAN' THE KITCHEN, THIS LADY 'BURNS'

It's not about with whom you want to share a romantic dinner, at a restaurant; it's about with who you want to run a house. After some time, passion takes a back seat to partnership. On the surface, dating seems romantic, but as I discussed in the first chapter, it's actually a time to preheat before the actual cooking begins. People must be honest when evaluating the real person in front of them, and have enough courage to be who they are in the beginning, so each person knows the other person. The grass is not always greener on the other side; its greener where you water it. The challenge is getting close enough to touch it and make sure it is actually grass and not turf.

There are people who create walls based on past relationships and experiences. You shouldn't bring old baggage into a new relationship. The baggage was made for traveling, it was not meant for you to have it monogrammed and keep with you. Don't create obstacles to a good relationship by turning every small interaction into a test. You can teach someone how to treat you, but testing them is not the way to do it. Teaching allows you to learn from the experience. When you test, you are the one who knows the answer you are looking for, and if you're dealing with someone who doesn't know you very well, you can't be upset with them, if they don't have the answer. Whether you're talking or listening, you need to be clear about why something's being said. Motive and message are important. Sometimes what you hear does not reflect the meaning behind the words.

My Grandmother never spanked me, but she said something to me one day when I tried to talk while she was speaking. "You shouldn't let your mouth open without proper adult supervision!"

I asked her what she meant, and she continued, "Only children speak over people, because they have a fear of not being heard. You shouldn't act childish and let that child in you run your life. As an adult you have the opportunity and the choice to act out of a place of fear or act out of a place of love."

I've met a good amount of people who say they are good at communicating; a few are in my same field of marketing and communications. I have found that what they should really say is that they are good at talking. Words are not communication; they are just a channel of communication.

Communication is sending a message in a way that it can be understood and receiving messages with clarity. Mood, tone, rate of speech, and active listening are all part of communicating. If you haven't reached the point where you can use and understand these elements, there will be miscommunication. While miscommunication finds its way into most relationships, good communicators find open channels and resolve the issue. If you have found yourself ignoring an issue or leaving it frustrated, it's because you reached the limit of your communication skills.

Don't give your power away. The pain of what happened is inevitable, but continuing to suffer is optional. Mistakes are the growing pains of wisdom. Most of the time people just need to be accepted, not forgiven. Your own life is the only life you can control. By constantly reliving the pain of what happened, you are giving your power away to the person who wronged you. It's not like you won't get upset anymore or ever feel anxious, but knowing that your emotions are just fleeting feelings, independent of YOU, will help ease your tension and allow room for positive feelings. Forgiveness is oftentimes the simple realization that there is nothing that actually needs to be forgiven. Working on a better you is more fulfilling than hanging on to contempt of others.

As women, we have the tendency to analyze far too much. There is a difference between baggage and intuition. If we meet someone who has many things on our list, but our gut is telling us, 'I don't trust this person,' that's more important than the list.

A large predictor on whether you have a relationship that will stand the test of time has less to do with how many sparks fly and more to do with the similarity of your expectations. Finding out what it would take for a person to commit is a good foundational question. The person being asked needs to have courage to answer and the person receiving the knowledge has to have courage to act on what you learn. You enter a situation knowing there may be some struggles, but kindness and courage are often overlooked qualities.   Pay attention to what he does for himself and what sacrifices he makes when spending his time. This will help you identify the things he values. Does he wake up early to get the gym or to be the first in line to have his car detailed? Does he remember to call the cable company to order the NFL ticket before football season starts? If you pay attention to what he is capable of doing for the things he values, you will have a good idea of what he is willing to commit if it meant he could lose you.

What's a better aphrodisiac than showing someone that you love them enough to prepare deliciously healthy foods? Do you know what could kill that romantic mood? Serving it at the table with the recipient while they are; in sweat pants, hair wrapped in a scarf, eau de funky, sagging pants, and dirty fingernails. Prepare as if you would be going out of the house and dress up! Shave. Put on lip gloss. You may feel like you shouldn't bother, but if you were going out you would dress up. Why? Are you trying to impress people you don't know? Surely you can do the same for the person whose heart you would like to keep. Sometimes we spend more efforts with people that are strangers in terms of making an impression that the person that is closest to us.

Divide up the tasks. One of you will be in charge of the menu and the other in charge of ambiance. For the décor, think candles, flowers, sweet smells, and romantic music. Clear up any clutter and hide anything that has Fisher-Price on it. Set a nice table with your nicest dishware or throw a blanket in front of the fireplace for a picnic.

If you are in charge of the menu, keep it simple. It needs to be hot, but not heavy! Studies show that spicy foods can raise your heart rate, cause flushing, and generally mimic some of the effects of sexual stimulation. For centuries, chilies and other heat-inducing ingredients have been added to love potions and other sensual aids to increase desire. The last thing you want, for your hot date, is to spend half the night slaving over the stove. Overeating will lead to an early retirement. Opt for simple, delicious bites of food, and earn bonus points for finger foods, to feed each other, of course.

For my sexy date night menu, I would start with a light arugula salad. Arugula has a peppery bite that makes it more exciting than lettuce, but it won't get in your teeth like spinach. Dress your salad up with different textures to tease the senses; crumbled feta cheese or candied pecans with a champagne vinaigrette.

For the main course, try THIS CHICK IS HOT TWEENST THE THIGHS (p. 75). It is easy to prepare, yet elegant to serve. You can make the sauce while the pasta cooks. The red pepper flakes give the dish just the right amount of heat, for a spicy evening.

Don't fuss making a fancy dessert. Put together a plate of indulgent bite-sized treats, like chocolate-covered strawberries, grapes and rich truffles. You don't want to be spending all evening in the kitchen, making supper, instead of spooning morsels into each other's mouths. Come to think of it, facing a train-wrecked kitchen after dinner can be a surefire mood killer as well.

# *HOW TO MAKE MENUS*

Planning your meals ahead of time takes the guess work out of dinner preparation and saves a lot of time. It's frustrating to start to prepare a meal after a long day of work or a full day monitoring children and realize you have to make a trip to the store before you can start dinner. My goal with this was to encourage people to start Meal Planning Monday to provide recipes that taste great, are easy to make, and encourage you to try your hand at creating a week's worth of home cooked meals no matter how busy you are.

If you don't have a plan, it's going to be very difficult to buy exactly what you need at the store. I know you have probably heard this a million times; shopping with a list will save you time and money when you're at the store. You're less likely to impulse buy when you are armed with a detailed list. I separate my grocery list into three columns: Menu, We Have, and We Need. This helps me stay focused and controls any panicking about forgetting something. The most important thing to keep in mind; be easy on yourself- things come up. I keep a few backup easy meals ready to go in the freezer or pantry. This could be a few extra pieces of chicken that I marinated and threw in the freezer while preparing for another day or, as easy as an extra jar of spaghetti sauce and bag of frozen ravioli that you reserve for emergency dinners, or when you're just plain too tired for something more involved.

I find it to be helpful to plan, not just my main dishes, but also my side dishes. This has helped me cut back on produce waste. I keep in mind some fresh items are more perishable than others. I used to just go and buy a bunch of fruits and vegetables and hope we could eat them all. Now I plan more carefully (grapes with Tuesday night's dinner, green salad on Monday and Wednesday) and I waste very few fruits and veggies. If I have bought cilantro at the store on Saturday, I make sure to use it in my meals by Tuesday, to prevent me from discovering it has gone bad or grown hairy before I am ready to use it.

My weekly menus in August will differ greatly from the ones in February, because I try to eat food when it is in season, which saves money and ensures an ever-changing variety of fresh ingredients. In-season produce is usually on sale (or free to be picked from my garden!) and helps me stick to a budget. I try to change my menu each month because my family likes variety. So we might only eat the same thing once a month. Your family might like something more predictable.

I have provided seven days' worth of great recipes that were tested in my own kitchen. They are truly easy to make, delicious and nutritious. Feel free to alter these to suit your family's tastes and needs. Years as a single mother on a budget taught me how to stretch my budget, and it serves well into my marriage. The main secret is that we try to limit my grocery visits to once a week. We usually do one larger grocery run per month to stock up on staples (the large superstores are great for this), and then 2-3 other grocery visits throughout the month to get items like fresh produce, juices and milk.

Another secret is that the staple items are part of planning ahead for recipes. I know that if I have a few certain ingredients in the house, I can whip up a quick meal without having to run to the grocery store. Also for these items, I have a general idea of what they normally cost. In the event they go on sale, I can stock up, occasionally using coupons, but not always.

I probably need to point out that I am not anti-coupon. I use some coupons myself. I think they can be a helpful tool. However, I don't believe in existing solely on groceries that can be purchased with coupons. I'm not convinced that doing this is responsible on a dietary level (It's very difficult to eat lots of raw produce and fresh meat when you only buy coupon items) or on an Earth-friendly level (It's very difficult to buy unpackaged groceries with a coupon).

I feed a family of four on a $350 per month budget, (including cleaning supplies, many name brand toiletries and paper products) without depending on coupons much at all. You don't have to become a coupon queen in order to get your grocery budget under control.

I am in Ohio, so local produce is available seasonally. My first goal is to buy local, accompanied with grocery store private label items. The quality has improved and often the value beats name brands. Private label products have come a long way, and I've been more than satisfied with almost all of my purchases.

Private label products don't require a huge marketing budget, which means that you're paying mostly for the food itself, not for the fancy ads. Plus, almost every private label item I've ever purchased has come with a money-back guarantee. Some even come with a double money-back guarantee, so there's little risk. I encourage you to give them a try! Even if you find something you don't care for now and then, odds are good that you'll find some things you enjoy, and that can help to keep your grocery budget down.

If your refrigerator doesn't have its own water filter built in, invest in a filtered water pitcher to keep in your fridge, as well as a bottle in taking to work. There's little nutritional benefit to drinking sweetened beverages (even fruit juice has some draw backs), so kick them to the curb, or at least reduce the amount you drink. I'd say the same for diet beverages. They provide nothing in the way of nutrition and don't hydrate like water. They're grocery budget fluff, and if you need to get serious about reducing your budget, this is a great place to start.

Stop wasting so much food. I know this is a challenge, but it is a waste for your wallet and for the atmosphere. Join me for Food Waste Fridays! Each Friday I check my refrigerator for leftovers and make a meal out of what I find. You will be amazed at how much money you can save by simply using up the food you buy.

One of the challenges with leftovers is remembering to eat them! It's easy to shove the containers to the back of the fridge and completely forget about them. I find that I need to take a quick visual inventory of my fridge every day or two, usually in the evening around snack time, so that I can keep track of what needs to be eaten.

This also helps me to keep track of my produce. When I scan my fridge, I look for fruits or vegetables that are on the brink of rot and try to incorporate them into our meals or snacks before it's too late.

Making lunch or sandwiches out of leftovers usually works better when you've had sort of a plain meal (i.e. grilled chicken, not enchiladas). Leftover meat and random vegetables can make a tasty sub or salad with very little effort.

Make every effort to buy ingredients and not meals. Buying foods that are ready to eat or almost ready to eat, have a 'prep tax' and often the stores are using the food right before it is due to go bad. Try to cook and prepare food yourself instead of paying a factory to do it for you. This will be cheaper and likely healthier as well.

On the following pages I have a grocery list to accommodate preparation for two weeks of recipes. I call this the MEAN & CLEAN menu because one week includes a week of recipes that include meat and the next week is meatless. I left each reader liberty to adjust quantities for their own portion size. Enjoy!

| **PRODUCE** | **BREAD** | Granola |
|---|---|---|
| Apples, Granny | Flat Bread | Corn Flakes/Rice |
| Apples, Gala | Tortillas | |
| Banana | Pizza Dough | **ETHNIC** |
| Pineapple | | Coconut Milk (both) |
| Strawberry | **MEAT/SEA** | Coconut Aminos |
| Spinach | Chicken, Whole | Coconut Oil |
| Kale | Chicken, Ground | Red Palm Oil |
| Cabbage | Turkey, Smoked | Chili Sauce (Thai) |
| Bok Choy | Turkey, Bacon | Seaweed |
| Shallot | Beef, Ground | Tahini |
| Onion, Green | Beef, Stew Meat | |
| Onion, Yellow/Rd | Bison, Ground | **CONDIMENTS** |
| Tomatoes | White Fish/wild | Dijon Mustard |
| Snap Peas | Salmon/wild Alask. | Ketchup |
| Broccoli | | Hot Sauce |
| Corn | **DAIRY** | Vinegar, Apple Cid |
| Avocado | Organic Butter | Vinegar, Rice Wine |
| Coconut | Cheese, Feta | Honey |
| Garlic | Cheese, Cheddar | Maple Syrup |
| Ginger | Cheese, Parm. | Almond Butter |
| Pepper, Green | Cheese, Cream | Peanut Butter |
| Pepper, Red | Milk, Coconut | Worcestershire |
| Pepper, Serrano | Milk, Almond | |
| Pepper, Jalapeño | Yogurt | **FROZEN** |
| Pepper, Habanero | | Corn |
| Potato, Red | **CEREAL** | Fruit, for smoothies |
| Potato, Sweet | Oats | Pineapple |
| Lettuce, Romaine | Grits | Peaches |
| **BAKING** | Oregano | **SEED/SNACK** |
| Sugar, Raw Cane | Paprika, Smoked | Almonds |
| Sugar, Brown | Parsley | Cashews |
| Flour, Gluten-Free | Pepper, Black | Sesame Seeds |
| Flour, All-Purpose | Sea Salt/Kosher | Sesame Strips |
| Flour, Coconut | Thyme | Hemp Seeds |

| | | |
|---|---|---|
| Flour, Chick Pea | Turmeric | Chia Seeds |
| Cornmeal | Vanilla, Extract | Raisins |
| Baking, Soda | Vanilla, Pod | Dried Cranberries |
| Baking, Powder | Oil, Canola | Pita Chips |
| Arrowroot Powder | Oil, Olive | Tortilla Chips |
| Allspice | Oil, Sunflower | |
| Basil | Milk, Evaporated | |
| Cardamon | Agave | |
| Cayenne | | |
| Chili Powder | **CAN FRUIT/VEG** | |
| Cilantro | Cannellini Beans | |
| Cinnamon | Beans, Red/Kidney | |
| Coriander | Beans, Black | |
| Curry, Jamaican | Tomato Paste | |
| Garlic Powder | Tomato Sauce | |
| Nutmeg | Mandarin Oranges | |
| Onion Powder | Applesauce | |

# MEAN

## SUNDAY

Breakfast

**COOL BREEZE SMOOTHIE**
Serves: 2

- ½ Cup water
- 4 Cups pineapple (3/4 of a medium pineapple)
- 2 fresh or frozen bananas
- 10 mint leaves
- 1 Tablespoons hemp/flaxseeds
- 1 Cup Spinach, tightly packed or 2 cups loosely packed (or any mild greens)
- ½ Cup Ice

Blend. Enjoy!

Brunch *(After church-great for snack & a nap)*

**DREAMY CREAMY GARLIC CHEESE GRITS**
Serves: 4

- 4 cups of water
- 2 tablespoons of organic coconut oil
- 6 small (1/2 pinky size) cloves of garlic, minced well, or to taste
- 1/2 cup of heavy cream (*see below, healthier-pureed canned cannellini beans)
- 1/2 teaspoon sea salt
- 1 cup of uncooked quick grits
- 2 cups of shredded organic cheddar cheese
- Additional salt and pepper, as needed
- Hot sauce, optional

Put the water on to boil. Melt the coconut oil in a small skillet. Add finely minced garlic and to the coconut oil, cooking just until transparent & tender. Remove and set aside.

*Pureed beans can offer the consistency you're missing in those comforting creamy soups. Use BPA-free canned cannellini beans; not only are the white beans the right hue when substituting for heavy cream, but their mild taste also won't overpower other flavors in your grits.

Just as the water is about to boil, turn down to medium and stir in the cream/cannellini beans. Add the salt, and then slowly (a little amount at a time) add in the grits, stirring constantly while adding them to the pot. When the grits begin to bubble, turn heat down to a medium low and simmer, stirring often, until mixture is thickened and creamy, about 5 minutes.

Add the garlic and coconut oil from the skillet and stir in the cheese. (Optional) This is a good time to wash out the skillet and start eggs! Cook the grits only long enough for the cheese to melt. Taste and adjust seasoning. Serve with a few dashes of hot sauce if desired. *HAVE LEFTOVERS? See snack for another day below.*

## GROOVY GRITS CAKES
Serves: "as many left over grits as you got!"

Preheat your deep fryer to 350F, or heat ½ Cup of coconut oil in a large skillet. In a medium bowl, mix up some flour with salt, pepper and Cajun Spice mix. Get out the container of leftover grits & slice however you like. I slice into squares & then triangles.
Dip them in the flour mixture.
Fry for 3-4 minutes. (You will know when they are done when they start floating)

Dinner

## ISLAND BEEF STEW

Serves: 6

- 2 lbs beef – cubed into 1 inch pieces
- 1/4 teaspoon salt
- 1/2 teaspoon Coconut Aminos (can substitute Worcestershire sauce)
- 1 tablespoon ketchup
- 2 cloves of garlic, thinly sliced and minced
- 1 teaspoon ginger, grated
- 2 tablespoon Coconut oil (Organic Red Palm Oil)
- 1 medium red onion, diced
- 2 Roma tomatoes, diced
- 1 tablespoon thyme
- 1 tablespoon brown sugar
- 2 1/4 cups water
- 1/4 teaspoon black pepper
- 1/4 scotch bonnet pepper, deseeded
- 1 green onion, chopped with tips
- 2 sprigs of fresh thyme (1 teaspoon dried)
- 1 carrot, diced
- 1 bag of frozen peas (fresh snap peas) optional

## COCONUT DUMPLINS

- 1/4 cup grated coconut
- 1 1/2 cups all-purpose gluten-free flour
- pinch of salt
- 1/2 cup cold coconut milk

Select cubed beef (about 1-2 inch pieces), then season with everything except the carrot, oil, water and brown sugar. Mix well and allow marinating a couple hours in the fridge.

Take beef out of the fridge about 15 minutes before you're ready to start cooking, you need it room temperature. In a deep (heavy) pot, heat the oil on high, then add the brown sugar and stir. IMPORTANT: Have the bowl with the seasoned beef close. Be aware- the sugar will start to melt, then go frothy and start taking on brown color. When it gets to a rich amber color (don't let it burn or go black or it will give the stew a bitter taste) start adding the marinated beef to the pot.

Use a spoon with a long handle in the event the melted sugar splashes up on you and be very gentle when adding the season beef to the pot. It's ok if the marinade gets in.

Stir well, turning each piece of beef until it is coated with a caramel color. With the heat still on high, bring it up to a boil. Then reduce to a simmer, cover the pot and let that go for about 15 minutes.

In the same bowl you marinated the beef, add the water and mix well to pick up any of the marinade which may have been left over. Add the water from the bowl as well as the diced carrot and bring to a boil. This will cook 1 hour.

After about 40 minutes you can start making the coconut dumplings. Make firm dough with the ingredients mentioned above. Set the dough ball to rest for about 10 minutes before shaping them into spinners.

Break off small pieces of the dough (about a tablespoon full) and using your hands, roll into a skinny cigar shape. Try to keep them the same size so they cook evenly.
The beef should be tender and have gravy. If there isn't enough liquid to cook the dumplings, add another cup or so of hot water to the pot before adding the raw dumplings. As it comes back to a full boil (raise the heat), start adding the dumplings to the pot. Stir in well (be gentle) so they are covered by liquid.

Reduce the heat to a simmer and let them cook for about 10 minutes. As the dumplings cook the flour helps to thicken the gravy, keep an eye on the pot so you're left with a bit of gravy. Top with some frozen peas (optional) taste for salt (adjust if needed) then turn off the stove, cover the pot and let the residual heat cook the peas

*Prepare for Monday:*
*next page

## HOT BERRY JAM
Yields: nearly 1 pint

- 1 tablespoon of fresh lemon juice
- 1 tablespoon apple cider vinegar
- 1 habanero pepper, seeded and minced
- 2 tablespoons arrowroot powder
- ¾ cup plus 3 tablespoons apple cider
- 2 cups organic raw cane sugar
- 1 pound medium organic strawberries, washed, dried, hulled & cut in half

Use a medium-size saucepan to combine the lemon juice, vinegar, and chile. Turn the heat to medium and simmer for about 1 ½ minutes, reducing the mixture until about 1 tablespoon remains. Remove from heat and set aside.

In a small bowl, combine the arrowroot powder with 3 tablespoons of apple cider and mix until the arrowroot powder has dissolved. Transfer to the saucepan with the lemon-vinegar –chile mixture and add the remainder of the apple cider, the sugar, and the strawberries.

Turn the heat to low and cook the mixture, stirring frequently, for about 5 minutes until all the sugar has dissolved. Raise the heat to medium low and simmer, without stirring, for 15 minutes. Remove from heat, stirring 5 times. Allow to cool. Pour or ladle into a sterilized canning jar & refrigerate.


## MONDAY
Breakfast

## MERRY MONDAY CAKES
Yields: 12 cakes
(Place metal mixing bowl in freezer while collecting ingredients)

- 1 ½ cups stone ground cornmeal
- ½ cup gluten free all-purpose flour (I like coconut flour, but absorbs 3 times more liquid than standard)
- 1 teaspoon baking powder

- 1 teaspoon fine sea salt
- ¼ teaspoon of cayenne pepper
- 2 ½ cups boiling almond milk
- 1 jalapeno, seeded and minced
- Extra virgin organic coconut oil

In a large bowl, mix cornmeal, flour, baking powder, salt & cayenne pepper. Set aside.

In a small saucepan, bring the almond milk to a boil then slowly stir into the bowl with cornmeal mixture. Add the jalapeno to the batter, mix well. Refrigerate the batter for 20 minutes. (optional)

Preheat oven to 200F

Warm a large, nonstick skillet or griddle over medium-high heat and grease well with 1 tablespoon of coconut oil. Add ¼ cup of batter to the skillet (I use gravy ladle) per cake, enough where they don't touch. After about 1 minute, when the bottom starts to set and you see first bubble, reduce heat and shape cakes by pushing to make ½ inch thick. Cook the cakes for 7 minutes each side, adding more oil after turning, until they are golden brown on each side. Transfer cooked cakes to baking sheet to keep warm until all batter is used. Serve with HOT BERRY JAM

Snack: Almonds

Dinner

## SKILLET FISH w/ GARLIC CILANTRO BUTTER
Serves: 4

- ¼ teaspoon sea salt
- ¼ teaspoon ground cumin
- ¼ teaspoon garlic powder
- ¼ teaspoon basil
- 1/8 teaspoon ground red pepper
- 4 (6-ounce) tilapia fillets
- Coconut cooking spray

- 1 organic lemon, quartered
- 2 tablespoons organic butter, softened
- 1 garlic clove finely minced
- 2 tablespoons finely chopped fresh cilantro
- 1/2 teaspoon grated organic lemon rind
- 1/4 teaspoon paprika
- 1/8 teaspoon sea salt

Combine first 5 ingredients; sprinkle over both sides of fish. Heat a large nonstick skillet over medium-high heat. Coat pan with coconut cooking spray. Coat both sides of fish with cooking spray; place in pan. Cook 5 minutes on each side or until fish flakes easily when tested with a fork or until desired degree of doneness. Place fish on a serving platter; squeeze lemon quarters over fish.

Place butter and remaining ingredients in a small bowl; stir until well blended. Serve with fish and emerald rice (below).

## EMERALD RICE
Serves: 4

- 2/3 cups organic chicken broth or vegetable broth
- 2 fresh poblano chiles, stems and seeds removed, and roughly chopped
- 10 sprigs cilantro, plus extra for garnish
- Sea salt, about 1/2 teaspoon if using salted broth, 1 teaspoon of Coconut Aminos
- 1 tablespoon olive oil
- 1 cup rice, preferably organic basmati
- 4 garlic cloves, peeled and finely chopped
- ½ cup organic grilled/frozen corn (optional add in)

The flavoring: In a 2-quart saucepan, combine the broth and chilies, bring to a boil, then partially cover and simmer gently over medium to medium-low heat for about 10 minutes, until the chilies are very soft. Pour the chili mixture into a food processor, add the cilantro (stems and all), and process to a smooth puree. Transfer to bowl and stir in the salt.

*The rice*: Using previous pan, add the oil and heat over medium. Add the rice and onion, and cook, stirring regularly, until the rice is chalky looking and the onion is soft, about 5 minutes. Stir in the garlic and cook a minute longer.

Add the warm chili liquid to the hot rice pan, stir once, scrape down any rice clinging to the side of the pan, cover, and cook over medium-low heat for 15-20 minutes. Uncover and check a grain of rice: It should be nearly cooked through. If the rice is just about ready, turn off the heat, re-cover and let stand for 5 to 10 minutes longer to complete the cooking. Fluff with a fork, add corn (optional) decorate with cilantro sprigs and it's ready to serve.

**\*\*HAVE LEFTOVER RICE?* SEE NOTE ON NEXT PAGE FOR LUNCH**


## TUESDAY
Breakfast


### PROTEIN MUFFIN NO FLUFFIN'
*Yields: 12 muffins*

- 2 mild chicken sausages, sliced or ¼ sleeve turkey sausage
- 1/4 cup red bell pepper, diced
- 1/4 cup carrots, grated
- 1/2 cup fresh spinach or kale, chopped
- 2 tablespoons fresh basil, diced
- 1/2 teaspoon sea salt
- 1/4 teaspoon fresh ground pepper
- 10 Large organic eggs

Preheat oven to 375 degrees. Thoroughly grease a 12-cup muffin pan with coconut oil.

In a skillet, cook sausage until cooked through and no longer pink. Thinly slice or break the sausage up into "crumb" size pieces.

In a medium bowl, combine cooked sausage, red bell pepper, shredded carrots, spinach, and basil. Set aside.

In a large bowl, whisk together eggs, salt and pepper. Add egg mixture to the sausage and veggie mixture and stir to combine.

Using a measuring cup or an ice cream scoop, fill muffin cups with egg mixture being sure not to fill cups to the rim. I used to 1/3 cup in each 'cup'.

Bake (GO GET DRESSED) the egg muffins for 20 to 25 minutes or until eggs are set in the middle. These can be refrigerated for up to 3 days in airtight container. Pop in microwave to reheat.

Snack: Raisins

Lunch

**ADD 2 teaspoons of sesame seeds to Monday's left over emerald rice, dampen hands, roll into balls. Warm in toaster oven on 350F for 10 minutes to accompany salad.

## ASIAN FUSION SALAD
Serves: 2

- ½ head Napa cabbage (5 oz) or package organic cole slaw mix
- 1 thinly sliced carrot
- 1 thinly sliced peeled cucumber
- 3 sheets toasted seaweed, sliced into strips
- 2 tablespoons toasted sesame strips
- 1/4 cup cilantro leaves
- 1 avocado, sliced, pit removed
- 1/3 cup Almonds

Add salad ingredients to a large mixing bowl. Set aside. Drizzle the vinaigrette over the salad and serve immediately.

## GINGER VINAIGRETTE DRESSING

- 2 tablespoons Rice Wine Vinegar
- 2 tablespoons Coconut Aminos
- 1/4 cup toasted sesame oil
- 1/4 cup sunflower/canola oil
- 2 tablespoons honey or brown sugar (use brown sugar for vegan)
- 2 cloves garlic, minced
- 1 tablespoon grated ginger
- 1 tablespoon toasted sesame seeds
- 1/2 teaspoon black pepper

To make the vinaigrette, place all ingredients in a jar, close tightly and shake vigorously to combine and emulsify.

Dinner
## NO-LIE NO FRY CHICKEN
Serves: 6

- 1 cup milk/milk substitute
- 3/4 cup organic balsamic dressing
- 3 tablespoons hot pepper sauce
- 2 tablespoons Dijon mustard
- 2 garlic cloves, minced
- 2 teaspoons salt
- 1/2 teaspoon ground black pepper
- 12 chicken pieces (breasts, thighs and drumsticks) skinless and bones
- 1 cup Corn Flakes/Rice Krispies
- 1/3 cup freshly grated Parmesan cheese
- 1/4 cup all- purpose flour
- 2 teaspoons dried thyme
- 1/2 teaspoon paprika
- 1/2 teaspoon cayenne pepper
- 3 tablespoons butter, melted

Whisk milk, balsamic dressing, hot pepper sauce, mustard, garlic, 1 teaspoon salt and 1/2 teaspoon pepper in large bowl to blend well. Add chicken and turn to coat. Cover; chill at least 1-2 hours turning chicken occasionally.

Place racks on 2 large rimmed baking sheets. Whisk breadcrumbs, cheese, flour, thyme, paprika, cayenne and 1 teaspoon salt in large baking dish to blend. Remove chicken from marinade, allowing excess to drip off. Add chicken to breadcrumb mixture and turn to coat completely. Arrange chicken, skin side up, on racks on baking sheets. Let stand 30 minutes.

Preheat oven to 425°F. Drizzle butter over chicken. Bake until crisp, golden and cooked through, about 50 minutes. Serve warm with new potatoes (below).

## NEW POTATOES
Serves: 4-6

- 1 1/2 pounds small red potatoes
- 1/8 cup olive oil
- 1 Apple Cider vinegar
- ½ teaspoon sea salt
- 1/2 teaspoon freshly ground black pepper
- 1 tablespoons minced garlic (3 cloves)
- 2 tablespoons minced fresh basil leaves

Preheat the oven to 400 degrees F.

Cut the potatoes in half or quarters and place in a bowl with the olive oil, salt, pepper, garlic and rosemary; toss until the potatoes are well coated. Dump the potatoes on a baking sheet and spread out into 1 layer; roast in the oven for at least 1 hour, or until browned and crisp. Flip twice with a spatula during cooking to ensure even browning.

Remove the potatoes from the oven, season to taste, and serve.

## WEDNESDAY
Breakfast

# EGGCELENT BREAK-FAST
Serves: 4

- 4 -8 large grass-fed organic eggs;
- 1 tablespoons coconut oil
- 4 slices of turkey bacon; cut into small pieces;
- 2 green onions, minced;
- ½ cup spinach, minced;
- 1 tsp. almond flour;
- ½ cup of chicken stock;
- 2 teaspoons fresh lemon juice;
- Sea salt and freshly ground black pepper to taste
- 4 small mason jars (can use 2-4, test by placing jars in large cooking pot, jar must sit flat on bottom)

Place skillet over medium-high heat, add the bacon and the coconut oil and cook for about 7 to 10 minutes, until brown.

Add the green onions and spinach to the turkey bacon and cook for another 3 to 5 minutes.
Add the almond flour and combine everything together, then add the chicken stock and lemon juice. Bring to a boil and cook until a nice texture is obtained.

Prepare 4 glass jars and rub some cooking fat on the bottom and inside edges. Pour some of the bacon and mushroom mixture evenly in each jar and break one or two eggs on top. Season with sea salt and freshly ground black pepper to taste.

Place the 4 mason jars into a big cooking pot, making sure they are stable and add water until it reaches the middle of your jars. (GO GET DRESSED) Bring to a medium-high heat and cook 15 to 20 min or until the eggs are cooked the way you like them.

Once the cooking is done, remove the glass jars from the pot using tongs, being careful not to burn yourself on the hot jars or dripping water. Set aside until cool enough to handle, sprinkle some green onion tops on top and serve.

Snack: Organic Yogurt

Lunch

## POTATO & ONION FLAT BREAD
Serves: 1-2

- 2 tablespoons olive oil
- 1 small yellow onion, thinly sliced into circles (can substitute sun ripened tomatoes)
- 1 red potato, peeled and thinly sliced (use left over potatoes from last night's dinner)
- 1 tablespoon whole rosemary needles
- 1 teaspoon sea salt
- 1/4 teaspoon black pepper
- Cornmeal for the baking sheet
- 1 flatbread

Heat oven or toaster oven to 400° F.

Heat the oil in a large cast-iron skillet over medium heat. Add the onion and cook until golden, 5 to 7 minutes. Transfer the onion to a bowl. Add the potato, rosemary, salt, and pepper and toss; set aside.

Lightly oil non-stick baking sheet and sprinkle the bottom with the cornmeal. Place the flat bread on the baking sheet/ pizza tin. Arrange the potato mixture evenly over the dough, leaving a 1-inch border. Bake until the crust is golden brown, about 10 minutes. Slice into wedges

Dinner

My Grandma always referred to the 'trinity' during her cooking. I had always thought she was blessing her food before cooking it until I got older & learned that it was a term endeared by her Southern roots.
My Trinity is 1 cup of chopped onion, 1/2 cup of chopped sweet green bell pepper or sometimes red or a combination of the two and 1/4 cup of chopped celery. When garlic is included, it is referred to as the Pope, or in Patois, *'wit da Pope'*.

# COUPLED UP MEATLOAF w/ TOMATO GRAVY
Serves: 4-6

- 1-1/2 pounds of Bison/very lean ground beef*
- 1 tablespoon of coconut oil
- 1 medium red onion, chopped fine
- 1/2 cup of green bell pepper, chopped fine
- 1 stalk (rib) of celery, chopped fine
- 3 cloves of garlic, minced
- 1/4 cup of organic butter
- 2 tablespoons of all-purpose flour (for the roux)
- 1 (15 ounce) can of tomato sauce
- 1 can of water
- 1 tablespoon of Coconut Aminos/Worcestershire sauce
- 1/2 cup of evaporated milk
- 1 large egg
- 1/2 cup of oatmeal with ½ teaspoon basil added
- 1/2 teaspoon of sea salt
- 1/4 teaspoon of freshly cracked black pepper
- Pinch of cayenne
- Additional flour, for coating
- 1 tablespoon of canola oil, for browning

Preheat the oven to 350 degrees F. Place the ground beef in a large bowl; set aside.

Heat the coconut oil over medium and cook the onion, bell pepper and celery until tender; add the garlic, cook for another minute, transfer to a plate to cool.

Wipe out the skillet, and add the 1/4 cup of canola oil. Heat over medium high heat and stir in the flour. Cook and stir until it is browned, remove from the heat, and let cool slightly. Slowly whisk in the tomato sauce, water and Coconut Aminos /Worcestershire and return to the heat. Bring to a boil, reduce heat and simmer for 15 minutes.

Whisk together the milk and egg; stir in the oatmeal and add that mixture to the ground bison/lean beef. Add the salt, pepper, cayenne and cooked veggies; mix gently and shape into a loaf. The mixture should be firm. If it is breaking apart, return to the bowl and additional bread crumbs until it holds together.

In a large, oven safe skillet, heat the tablespoon of oil over medium high heat. Carefully transfer the meatloaf to the skillet and sear on all sides, turning carefully. Pat any cracks that form back together.

*Note*: You can skip the searing process if you prefer. Once all sides have browned, pour the tomato gravy over the meatloaf and transfer the entire skillet to a 350 degree F oven for about 1 hour, basting occasionally.

## THURSDAY
Breakfast

### BANANA CRANBERRY SMOOTHIE

- 1/2 cup frozen organic cranberries
- 1 small ripe banana, peeled, sliced
- 1 cup cold Coconut & Almond Milk/non-dairy milk
- A splash of cranberry juice
- 2 tablespoons raw organic honey, to taste
- 1-2 tablespoons vanilla rice protein powder, to taste

Combine the ingredients in a blender, cover and blend on a lower speed to process the cranberries. Add an ice cube or two if you like it super cold. Feel the cranberry love.

Lunch

### APPLE-A-DAY CRUNCH AWAY SANDWICH

- 1 gala apple, cored and sliced into rings
- Up to 1 tablespoon Almond butter
- Granola

Generously spread almond butter on one apple slice. Sprinkle granola over almond butter and top with another apple slice. Repeat using remaining apple slices and almond butter.

Dinner
## OLE' & AWAY  (Crock pot chicken tacos)
Serves: 4

- 1½ pounds chicken breasts
- ½ pound dried pinto beans/black beans
- 1 ½ cups water
- 1 ounce taco seasoning (see below if not premade)
- 1 16-ounce jar of your favorite salsa  (see below if not premade)
- For serving: tortillas or taco shells and your choice of optional toppings, such as shredded lettuce, chopped tomatoes, shredded cheese, black beans, corn, chopped avocados or guacamole,  and hot sauce

Wash the beans and soak overnight in cold water. Drain the beans and dump into slow cooker.
Place chicken in the crock-pot & add water.
Sprinkle taco seasonings over chicken.
Pour salsa on top.
Cook on low (for 6-8 hours) or high (for 4 hours).
Just before serving, use two forks to shred the chicken.
Stir to evenly distribute salsa throughout chicken. Serve immediately with desired toppings.


## TACO SEASONING MIX
Yields: 1 ounce

- 1 tablespoon chili powder
- 1/4 teaspoon garlic powder
- 1/4 teaspoon onion powder
- 1/4 teaspoon crushed red pepper flakes
- 1/4 teaspoon dried oregano
- 1/2 teaspoon paprika
- 1 1/2 teaspoons ground cumin
- 1 teaspoon sea salt
- 1 teaspoon black pepper

## CHUNKY SALSA
Yields: 4 servings

- 3 tomatoes, chopped
- 1/2 cup finely diced onion
- 3-4 serrano chiles, finely chopped
- 1/2 cup chopped fresh cilantro
- 1 large clove of fresh garlic, minced
- 1 teaspoon salt
- 2 teaspoons lime juice

In a medium bowl, stir together tomatoes, onion, garlic, chili peppers, cilantro, salt, and lime juice. Chill for one hour in the refrigerator before serving.

**FRIDAY-** No waste Friday (do left overs first)
Breakfast

## NUTTER BUTTER BANANA QUESADILLA
Serves: 2-4

- Coconut oil cooking spray or butter
- 2 tablespoons natural creamy peanut butter
- 2 whole grain tortillas
- 1 large ripe banana, sliced
- 4-5 strawberries, sliced
- 1/8 teaspoon cinnamon (optional)
- 1/8 teaspoon Nutmeg (optional)

Heat a medium non-stick skillet over medium high heat and spray pan with coconut oil cooking spray.
Spread 1 tablespoon of the peanut butter evenly over each tortilla. Arrange both the banana and strawberry slices over one tortilla, sprinkle with a pinch of cinnamon, nutmeg, and top with the remaining tortilla, peanut butter side down. Press gently to help them stick together.
When the skillet is hot, add the quesadilla, flipping once, until golden brown, about 2 minutes per side. Cut each quesadilla into quarters.

Lunch

## SOULGOOD SUSHI ROLLS

Serves: 8

- 16 ounces cream cheese, softened  (*vegan substitute below)
- 1/2 cup salsa, plus more for dipping
- 1 tablespoon chili powder
- 1/4 teaspoon salt
- 1 avocado, thinly sliced
- 1 tablespoon lime juice
- 6 (8-inch) flour tortillas
- 1 ½ cups fresh baby spinach
- 2 medium carrots, long strips/ organic bag of matchstick carrots
- 1 red bell pepper, cut into thin strips
- 1 yellow bell pepper, cut into thin strips

In a medium bowl, combine the cream cheese, salsa, chili powder, and salt. In a separate small bowl, lightly sprinkle the avocado with the lime juice to prevent browning.

Trim round of each tortilla to make a roughly 6-1/2-inch square. Spread 3 tablespoons of the cream cheese mixture on a tortilla. Arrange 2 rows of spinach in the center of the tortilla, top them with a row each of red pepper, yellow pepper, carrots, and avocado. Roll the tortilla up tightly and wrap it in plastic wrap. Repeat for the remaining tortillas. Refrigerate the rolls for at least 1 hour and up to 6 hours.

Right before serving, slice the rolls crosswise into 1/2-inch pieces and spoon extra salsa into a bowl for dipping.

## OH BOY, NO SOY VEGAN CREAM CHEESE (Vegan)

Yields: 1 Large Cup    (with wait time, takes a day and a half. I start on Fridays)

- 1 1/2 cups raw cashew halves, soaked for 10 hours
- 1/4 cup raw organic apple cider vinegar
- 2 tablespoons fresh lemon juice
- 2-3 tablespoons water

Place raw cashew halves in a glass dish (I like to see any debris) and fill with filtered water. Cover and place in the fridge to soak for 12 hours.
Then, drain and rinse the cashews with water.

Drop cashews in a blender or food processor and add remaining ingredients. Begin with 2 tablespoons of water and work up to 3 tablespoons if needed. The water is in the recipe just to help the mixture get as smooth as possible in the blender.

Blend for 2 minutes or so, until it's as smooth as smooth can be. Set aside for a couple of hours.

Drape a tall plastic container with cheesecloth. For thinner, more creamy cream cheese, I double up the cloth. For a firmer cheese, use 2-ply.

Spoon the cream cheese mixture onto the cheesecloth.

Pull up the sides of cheesecloth and tie tightly with a piece of string or twine.

Hang the cheese bag on a kitchen utensil (I use a wooden spoon) and rest it inside a vase or juice pitcher. It just has to be extended in the air so that the extra liquids can drain from it.

Leave in a warm place for at least 24 hours-quite a bit of liquid should have drained by then. Then, remove from the hanging setup you've created, remove cheesecloth and serve as is or add flavors such as herbs, vanilla or a touch of sugar.

Dinner

## **BEANS CHASING RICE**

- 1 tablespoon of butter or oil
- 1/2 pound of Andouille or other smoked chicken sausage, chopped
- 1 slice of smoked turkey
- 1 cup of chopped red onion
- 1/2 cup of chopped green or red bell pepper, or use a combination
- 1/4 cup of chopped celery
- 1 tablespoon of minced garlic
- 2 cups of vegetable stock or broth
- ¼ teaspoon of basil (I use fresh, cut to half if dried)
- ¼ teaspoon thyme
- ¼ teaspoon sage
- 1/4 to 1/2 teaspoon of Cajun seasoning mix (below) or to taste
- 1/4 teaspoon of freshly cracked black pepper
- 1 large bay leaf
- 2 or 3 (15.5 ounce) cans of light or dark red kidney beans, rinsed and drained
- 2 cups of organic rice (I use Basmati)

Heat the oil in a large non-stick skillet (w/ lid)over medium high heat. Add the sausage until lightly browned, about 4 minutes.
Add the onion, bell pepper, and celery; cook and stir until vegetables are tender, about 5 minutes. Add the garlic and cook, stirring constantly, another 2 minutes.
 Add vegetable broth, fresh herbs, Cajun spice mix (below), pepper and bay leaf. Bring to a boil.

If making beans cream style, drain, rinse and mash a third can. Add it in here with the other two beans and rice, stir together well, reduce heat to medium low and cook, covered for 10 minutes, or until rice is tender. Fluff with a fork, taste and adjust seasonings as needed; serve immediately.

## CAJUN SPICE MIX
Yields: ¼ cup

- 1 teaspoons sea salt
- 2 teaspoons garlic powder
- 2 ½ teaspoons smoked paprika
- 1 teaspoon ground black pepper
- 1 teaspoon onion powder
- 1 teaspoon cayenne pepper
- 1 1/4 teaspoons dried oregano
- 1 1/4 teaspoons dried thyme
- 1/2 teaspoon red pepper flakes

## <u>SATURDAY</u>
Brunch
## HASH IT OUT w/ LEGS & EGGS
Serves: 4

- 2 tablespoons coconut oil
- 1 cup diced yellow onions
- 1/2 teaspoon minced garlic
- 1/2 cup diced red bell peppers
- 2 sweet potatoes, baked for 30 minutes at 400 degrees F, cooled, peeled and diced (3 cups)
- 2 cups diced smoked turkey leg
- 2 1/2 teaspoons sea salt, plus more for seasoning eggs
- 1 teaspoon fresh ground black pepper, plus more for seasoning eggs
- 1/4 cup turkey or chicken broth
- 1/4 cup BPA-Free canned coconut cream/milk (no low fat)
- 2 tablespoons coconut oil
- 4 large eggs

In a large nonstick saute pan, heat the coconut oil over moderately-high heat.

Add the onion, garlic and red pepper and cook, stirring, until softened and beginning to brown, 3 to 5 minutes. Add the sweet potatoes, turkey, salt and pepper and cook, stirring occasionally, until the potatoes are beginning to brown, about 6 to 8 minutes. Add the broth, coconut cream and cook for another 2 to 3 minutes, scraping up any brown bits that may have formed on bottom of pan. Keep warm in oven while frying eggs.

I prefer my eggs scrambled, but my man likes them fried. In a large, nonstick saute pan, melt the butter over medium high heat. When the butter is foamy, carefully crack the eggs into the pan and season lightly with salt and pepper. Reduce the heat to medium-low, cover and cook until the whites are firm, 2 to 3 minutes.

Divide the hash equally between 4 warm plates, remove the eggs from the pan, and divide the eggs between the plates. Serve with kale drizzled with olive oil.

Dinner
Homemade pizza on Fridays is one of my all-time favorite things to do-single with my boys or married with my honey. It is cheap, easy and, in my opinion, tastes way better than anything you can get delivered. Turn on some jazz then get in the kitchen TOGETHER to make some gourmet pizzas. When your pizzas come out of the oven, turn down the lights, light some candles and enjoy your Soul Food Italian cuisine picnic-style in the comfort of your own living room!

## BARBEQUE CHICKEN PIZZA

Prepared pizza dough (uncooked)

Sauce: (I have a great fresh home-made tomato sauce recipe below)
- 1 Tablespoon. minced garlic
- 1 small can tomato paste
- 1 medium BPA –free can tomato sauce
- 1 Large tomato, finely chopped
- 2 teaspoons fresh basil
- 2 teaspoons fresh oregano or 1 ½ dried
- Sea salt and pepper, to taste
- 2 Tablespoon fresh chopped cilantro
- 1 cup BBQ sauce (see BOSS SAUCE)

Toppings:

- about a handful of fresh chopped basil/cilantro
- 2 to 3 cups of mixed organic cheddar and mozzarella cheese
- 2 chicken breasts grilled in BBQ Sauce, then sliced
- 1 cup fresh pineapple – drained

For the Sauce: Brown garlic in a little olive oil in the bottom of a sauce pan. Add everything else, except the BBQ sauce, and simmer for 20 minutes. Then remove from heat and stir in the BBQ sauce.

Roll your pizza dough onto a pizza pan or pizza stone. Spread the sauce evenly over the pizza dough. Then top with cheese and pineapple. Bake in the oven at 400 degrees for 18 min. After cooking, top with grilled chicken slices and fresh chopped cilantro.

## TOMATO SAUCE

This is something I tend to do in August/September depending on how tomato season & my weekends look. If I were to choose quality time with my family & jars of tomato sauce…tomatoes get the can!

Yields: 4 pints

- 8 lbs. supremely ripe tomatoes (a bit overripe isn't bad here either)
- 1 teaspoon. sea salt
- 2 Tablespoons of fresh garlic, minced
- 1 Tablespoon of fresh basil
- 2 teaspoons of fresh oregano
- 1 small red onion, diced
- 4 Tablespoons fresh lemon juice
- 4 pint size jars with sealable lids for canning

Rinse the tomatoes clean and pat them dry. Wash your hands to remove the seeds and skin. I do this by
whirling the tomatoes on the pulse setting of a blender and push the puree through a fine sieve.

Put the peeled and seeded tomatoes or tomato puree, garlic, basil, onion, and oregano in a pot with the salt and bring to a boil. Reduce heat to a simmer and cook, stirring now and again, until the mixture is reduced by about a third, about 45 minutes.

Meanwhile, sterilize the jars and lids. My dishwasher has a 'sanitize' setting. I let it run through rinse to remove any soap, or you can bring a canning kettle full of water to a boil.

Put 1 Tbsp. of the lemon juice in each of the 4 jars. Transfer the hot tomato sauce to the hot jars, leaving about 1/2 inch of head space at the top. Screw on the lids, put the jars in a canning rack, and lower them into the boiling water in the canning kettle. Process sauce in jars for 40 minutes.

Remove jars and let them cool. Store in a cool, dark place (a cupboard or pantry are ideal) until ready to use.

## BANANA FRITTERS & FRINGE

Serves: 4

- 1 cup ground almonds
- 1/2 cup desiccated coconut (or fresh coconut, flaked & browned in 2 teaspoons butter)
- 2 tablespoons organic cane brown sugar
- 1 teaspoon cinnamon
- 6 bananas, peeled
- 1 egg white, beaten
- coconut cooking spray (Trader Joes)

If you aren't a fan of coconut, I understand. I used to hate coconut when I was younger, but over the years I've developed a taste for it - so long as it's not overkill. It's much better toasted, but of course you can just leave it out too. I keep coconut in the freezer so I always have some on hand. Just toss a couple of tablespoons into a hot skillet and keep it moving so it doesn't burn. It'll only take a few minutes.

Preheat oven to 350F.
Combine almond meal with the coconut (if fresh coconut-let it cool), brown sugar and cinnamon.

Brush bananas with egg white and coat with crumb mixture.

Place on lined baking sheets and spray with vegetable oil. Bake for 10 minutes until golden brown. Great with ice cream!!!!

# CLEAN

## SUNDAY
Brunch

### HOT n HARDY CHICK PEA PANCAKES
Yields: 10 pancakes Serves: 5-8

- 2 cups chickpea/besan flour
- 1 cup water
- ½ teaspoons- 1 tsp ground coriander
- 2 tablespoons nutritional yeast
- ½ cup fresh spinach, washed and excess water squeezed out
- 3 tomatoes, chopped into small pieces
- 3 green chilies, finely chopped
- 4-5 green onions, chopped
- ¼ cup carrots, shredded
- 3 garlic cloves, minced
- ¼ teaspoon chili powder
- sea salt, to taste
- extra virgin olive oil for cooking, if needed

Use a large non-stick skillet (add a small amount of oil if needed) and place on medium-low heat.
Add all ingredients into a large bowl and stir well until everything is fully mixed. Once the skillet is heated, get out a ¼ or ⅓ measuring cup to scoop up the batter and add into the pan. I flattened each pancake slightly with the back of a spatula right after pouring it into the skillet.

Cook for a few minutes on each side. Once the edges become crispy and turn a bit more of a brownish color, you should be able to easily flip it over. The other side will take less time to cook. Place on a cooling rack or baking tray while you cook the rest of the pancakes.

Eat on their own with fried apples, chutney...or add cheese in a sandwich. I haven't tried freezing these, but I'm sure they will freeze well.

## FRIED APPLES
Serves: 2-3

- 2 large granny smith apples
- 4 tablespoons real butter, sliced or 4 tablespoons organic virgin coconut oil
- Juice of ½ lemon
- 2 tablespoons raw organic cane sugar
- 2 tablespoons organic brown sugar
- 1 teaspoon cinnamon
- ¼ teaspoon nutmeg

Peel, core and cut apples into even slices.
Melt butter/coconut oil in skillet over medium heat.
Add apples and drizzle them with lemon juice.
Let apples simmer until most of butter is absorbed and apples are tender. (do not overcook. Apples should be firm to the touch, yet tender with a little give to the bite.)
Mix both sugars and sprinkle them over apples.
Toss to combine.
Lower heat if needed. Let apples cook until sugars are completely dissolved and syrupy.
Remove from heat and sprinkle apples with cinnamon. Toss to distribute cinnamon and nutmeg. Plate apples and serve hot!

## MONDAY
Breakfast

## MONDAY MORNIN MATCHA

- 2 bananas, frozen
- 1 cup Coconut or Almond Milk
- matcha powder - a few teaspoons to a few tablespoons depending on your matcha
- 1 vanilla bean, scraped from about 1-inch of the pod, do not use extract
- a few handfuls of ice
- honey, agave, or sweetener of choice (optional)

Blend everything together. Taste & adjust sweetener to your liking. If you're new to matcha – it's very finely ground, high quality, green tea powder. It's sweeter than steeped green tea and is super healthy because all of those amazing green tea antioxidants are more concentrated.

Lunch

## SWEET TART SPINACH SALAD
Serves: 5

- 8 ounces of organic fresh baby spinach
- 1/3 cup(s) bottled poppy seed salad dressing
- 1/2 lemon
- 1 BPA free can(s) (11-ounce) Mandarin orange sections, drained
- 1/2 cup(s) honey-roasted sliced almonds

*Dressing*
Serves: 4

- 2 teaspoons extra-virgin olive oil
- 1 shallot, finely chopped
- 1/4 cup cider vinegar
- 2 tablespoons pure maple syrup
- Salt & freshly ground pepper, to taste

Place spinach in large salad bowl. Drizzle dressing on top; squeeze juice from lemon half over salad. Just before serving, toss to combine and top with orange sections and almonds.

Heat oil in a small skillet over medium-low heat. Add shallot and cook, stirring, until softened, about 4 minutes. Add vinegar and maple syrup and bring to a boil. Season with salt and pepper.

Dinner

## RED HOT QUINOA BURGER
Serves: 6

- 1 small sweet potato, baked
- 1/4 cup quinoa
- 1/4 cup dry barley
- 15-ounce BPA-free can garbanzo beans, rinsed and drained
- 2 tablespoons parsley
- 1 teaspoon cayenne pepper
- 1 1/2 teaspoon oregano
- 1/2 teaspoon salt
- 1/2 teaspoon pepper
- 2 tablespoons whole wheat flour
- 2 tablespoons olive oil
- 1 1/2 fresh red peppers

Preheat oven to 400°F. Bake the sweet potato for 45-60 minutes or until soft. While the sweet potato is baking, cook the quinoa (20 mins) and barley in salted water in separate pots until soft, about 30-60 minutes (barley takes a little longer).

Remove the stem and seeds from the red peppers. Cut the whole pepper in quarters and the half a pepper in half, and roast all six pieces in the oven for about 15-20 minutes.

Once the sweet potato is baked and cooled, combine garbanzo beans, sweet potato, parsley, cayenne pepper, oregano, salt and pepper, flour, and one tablespoon oil in a food processor.

Allow the grains to cool, and then in a separate bowl, mix the bean mixture with the quinoa and barley.

Heat the remaining tablespoon of oil in a large pan on medium heat. Place heaping spoonful of the mixture onto the hot pan, and use the back of the spoon to pat them flat and form four-inch diameter patties. Brown both sides of each burger. Serve on a bun with one piece of the roasted pepper, sliced into thirds.

# TUESDAY
*Breakfast*

## GROWN FOLKS OATS
Serves: 4

- 2cups water
- 2 cups almond milk (or other non-dairy milk)
- 1 cup uncooked steel-cut oats
- 2 large bananas, mashed (1 cup mashed) or 1 cup applesauce
- 2 teaspoons ground cinnamon
- Pinch of salt
- 1 tablespoons ground hemp seeds
- 2 teaspoons vanilla extract

In a medium-sized pot, bring the water and almond milk to a boil. Add in steel-cut oats and a pinch of salt and reduce heat to low.

Stir in the mashed banana or applesauce (mashing helps disperse the sweetness throughout), ground hemp seeds. Simmer on low, uncovered, for 20-25 minutes, stirring every 5 mins or so.

When the oats are creamy and tender, remove from heat and stir in cinnamon to taste and pure vanilla extract. Serve immediately or allow cooling before transferring into air tight containers in the fridge. In the morning, add a splash of milk and reheat in the micro or on the stove top.


Lunch

## SKINNY DIP w/ PITA CHIPS
Yields: 2 ½ cups or 10 servings

### *CROCK POT CHICK PEACE*
- 7 cups water
- 1 pound dry organic chickpeas, sorted and rinsed
- 1/4 teaspoon baking soda
- Special equipment: a 2 1/2-quart crock pot

Place the water, chickpeas, and baking soda in a 2 1/2-quart slow cooker. Cover and cook on high heat for 4 hours, or on low heat for 8 to 9 hours, or until tender. Drain and serve immediately, or cool and use for hummus.

- 1 pound Crock Pot Chickpeas, cooled, recipe above*
- 1/3 cup tahini, stirred well
- 5 tablespoons freshly squeezed lemon juice
- 2 cloves garlic, minced
- 1 1/2 teaspoons sea salt
- 1/4 cup water
- 1/4 cup extra-virgin olive oil, plus extra for serving
- **Powdered sumac, optional

Place the lemon juice and water in food processor-process for 20 seconds. Add the tahini. Process for 20 seconds, scrape down the sides of the bowl. Add the chickpeas, garlic, and sea salt in the bowl of a food processor-process for one minute. Stop, scrape down the sides of the bowl, and process for another one minute. With the processor running, drizzle in the olive oil. Serve with Pita chips & Fresh sliced veggies.

* Recipe can be swapped with Black Beans, I add 1/3 cup cilantro and 2 jalapeños, deseeded &minced.
**Sumac is a Middle Eastern Spice and is often difficult to find (I get from a local Halal store, but you can mix lemon zest, black pepper/paprika for a similar taste)

Dinner
(on next page)

## SPICY SESAME NOODLES
Serves: 8

- 1 (16 ounce) package linguine pasta
- 6 cloves garlic, minced
- 2 teaspoons ginger, minced
- 6 tablespoons raw organic sugar
- 6 tablespoons safflower oil
- 6 tablespoons rice vinegar
- 6 tablespoons Coconut Aminos
- 2 tablespoons sesame oil
- 2 teaspoons chili sauce (Dark Star Organic)
- 5 green onions, sliced

- 1 teaspoon sesame seeds, toasted
- Organic broccoli crowns, steamed (optional)

Bring a pot of lightly salted water to high boil. Add pasta, and cook until al dente, about 8 to 10 minutes. Drain, toss with ½ teaspoon sesame oil and transfer to a serving bowl.

Meanwhile, place a saucepan over medium-high heat. Stir in garlic, ginger, sugar, oil, vinegar, coconut aminos, sesame oil, and chili sauce. Bring to a boil, stirring constantly, until sugar dissolves. Pour sauce over linguine, and toss to coat. Garnish with green onions and sesame seeds. I add steamed broccoli.

## RASCALLION PANCAKES
Yields: 4-8 servings

- 2 cups all-purpose flour, plus more for dusting
- 1/2 teaspoon coarse sea salt
- 1 cup boiling-hot water
- 3 to 4 Tablespoons vegetable oil (I love rice bran oil if you find it)
- 3 teaspoon toasted sesame oil
- 2 cups spring onions, green parts only, thinly sliced
- Coarse salt

Stir together flour, salt, hot water, and 1 tablespoon vegetable oil. You can also use a food processor with a dough blade.
Transfer to a lightly floured surface. Knead dough until soft and smooth and forming a round ball, 5 minutes. Cover with plastic wrap and a warm towel; let stand 20 minutes.

Divide dough into four pieces and roll each piece out (if you do not have rolling pin, I turn a metal mixing bowl over onto the rim & spread the dough over the rounded bottom of the bowl) making an 8-inch circle, keeping remaining pieces covered as you work.

Brush round with sesame oil. Starting on one end, roll each piece into a tight cylinder; pinch ends to seal. Press to flatten into an 8-inch disk again.

Brush with another layer of sesame oil, sprinkle with scallions, roll up into a tube and then into a spiral, flatten and again roll out gently into a slightly smaller sized disk.
Repeat with remaining dough pieces.

Heat 1 tablespoon vegetable oil in a 12-inch skillet over medium-high heat until oil is shimmering. Cook pancakes, flipping once, until golden, 2 to 3 minutes per side (add oil as necessary). Drain on paper towels.

Season with salt. (To keep warm, place in an oven heated to 200 degrees.) Cut into wedges, and serve with dipping sauce. (below)

## COCO GINGER SAUCE

- 1/4 cup Coconut Aminos
- 1/4 cup Chinese rice vinegar
- 1/4 cup sliced scallions
- 1 teaspoon minced ginger
- 1 teaspoon red pepper flakes
- ½ teaspoon raw organic sugar

## WEDNESDAY
*Breakfast*

## PEACHES N GINGER CREAM SMOOTHIE
Yields: 1 Serving

- 1 cup coconut/almond milk
- 1 cup peaches (frozen)
- 2 tablespoons maple syrup(Grade A)/honey
- 1/2 tsp fresh ginger (grated)

Blend & enjoy!

Lunch (next page)

## BETTA FETA SALAD
Serves: 4

- 1 ½ cup cooked/1 can organic chickpeas, rinsed and drained
- 2 avocados, pitted, and chopped
- 1 cup cooked organic sweet corn, cooled
- 1/3 cup chopped cilantro
- 2 tablespoons green onion
- 1/3 cup feta cheese
- Juice of 1 lime
- Salt and black pepper, to taste

In a medium bowl, combine chickpeas, avocado, sweet corn, cilantro, green onion, feta cheese, and lime juice. Stir until mixed well. Season with salt and pepper. Serve.

Dinner

## LENTIL BITS OF LOVE STEW
Serves: 4-6

- 2 Tablespoons olive oil
- 1 large white onion, chopped
- 1 teaspoon cumin seeds
- 1/4 teaspoon ground cardamom
- 1 teaspoon garlic, minced
- 2 Tablespoons fresh ginger, minced
- 2 teaspoons turmeric
- 1/2 fresh jalapeño, peeled, seeded, and minced
- 3 ½ cups vegetable stock
- 2 cups red lentils, rinsed
- 1 14-ounce BPA-free can fire-roasted crushed tomatoes
- 1/2 teaspoon sea salt
- 1 Tablespoons hemp seeds/Chia seeds
- 4 Tablespoons fresh chopped cilantro
- Cooked brown rice, for serving (optional)

Heat oil in a large saucepan over medium heat. Add onion and sauté until lightly caramelized, about 8 minutes. Add cumin seeds, cardamom, and garlic; sauté until fragrant, about 2 minutes.

Stir in 4 cups water, ginger, turmeric, jalapeño, vegetable stock, lentils, and tomatoes and bring to a boil. Reduce heat to low, cover, and simmer, stirring occasionally, until lentils are tender, about 15 minutes. Stir in salt, hemp/chia seeds, and cilantro; serve immediately with brown rice on the side, if using.

## CRANBERRY CORNBREAD
Serves: 10 Yields: 12 Muffin Cups

- 2 cups fine whole-grain cornmeal (less gluten-Bobs Red Mill)
- 3/4 cup whole-wheat pastry flour or white whole-wheat flour (Bobs Red Mill or King Arthur's)
- 1 teaspoon baking powder
- 1 teaspoon baking soda
- 1/4 teaspoon sea salt
- 2 large eggs
- 1 ½ cups buttermilk/ (1 Tablespoon vinegar+1 ½ cup coconut milk)
- 1/3 cup coconut oil, melted
- 1/2 cup honey
- 1 tablespoon finely grated orange zest
- 3/4 cup fresh cranberries, rinsed and patted dry, or frozen (not thawed)
- 1/3 cup dried cranberries

Preheat oven to 400°F. Coat a 9-inch metal cake pan with cooking spray.

Set aside 2 tablespoons cornmeal in a small bowl. Whisk the remaining cornmeal, whole-wheat flour, baking powder, baking soda and salt in a large bowl. Lightly whisk eggs in a medium bowl, then whisk in buttermilk/coconut milk+vinegar, oil, honey and orange zest until smooth. Make a well in the center of the dry mixture. Pour in the wet ingredients and stir with a spatula until just combined. Do not overmix; the batter should look lumpy.

Toss fresh and dried cranberries with the reserved cornmeal. (This will prevent the fruit from sinking to the bottom during baking.) Gently fold the cranberries and cornmeal into the batter. Scrape the batter into the prepared pan.

Bake the cornbread until the edges turn golden brown and a toothpick inserted into the center comes out with a few moist crumbs, 25 to 30 minutes. Let stand for 10 minutes before cutting into wedges. Best warm!

## THURSDAY

*Breakfast*

## SCRAMBLED VEGAN EGGS

- 4 teaspoons organic coconut oil, divided
- 5 Tablespoons chickpea flour (aka garbanzo bean flour)
- 6 Tablespoons water
- 1 green onion, chopped
- ¼ cup fresh mushrooms, chopped (not canned, too rubbery)
- ¼ cup kale, chopped
- sea salt or Indian black salt, to taste (I used about ¼ teaspoon gives more egg sulfur taste)
- Pinch tumeric
- Pinch black pepper, to taste

Heat two teaspoons of coconut oil in a small non-stick skillet.
In a small bowl, mix the chickpea flour with the water, scallion, and a couple pinches of turmeric, black salt or regular sea salt and pepper.

Add the fresh mushrooms into the skillet, and let them cook for about three minutes.
Add the remaining two teaspoons of coconut oil to the pan.

Pour the chickpea/scallion mix into the skillet, and let it cook without touching it for 3-5 minutes, or until you see the perimeter begin to 'set'.

Sprinkle the chopped kale into the skillet. Using a spatula, begin breaking the mix into smaller bite-size pieces.
Heat the 'eggs' until they are cooked through (no batter in sight).
Salt and pepper to taste.


Lunch
**VEGGIE WRAP** (wrap your favorite veggies in a tortilla)


Dinner

## MUAH! FOR QUINOA
Serves: 2-4

- 1 cup quinoa
- 1/2 tsp. kosher salt, divided
- 2 Tablespoons olive oil
- 1 small red onion, chopped
- 2 cloves garlic, minced
- 1 medium organic zucchini, chopped (about 2 cups)
- 3 large organic carrots, peeled and chopped (about 1 1/2 cups)
- 2 tsp. fresh thyme
- 1/4 tsp. crushed red pepper flakes
- 1/4 tsp. ground black pepper
- 1 Tbsp. chopped fresh green onion

Rinse quinoa in a strainer. In a heavy-bottomed saucepan, bring quinoa, 2 cups water, and 1/4 tsp. salt to a boil. Cover, reduce heat, and simmer until quinoa absorbs the water, 10 to 15 minutes.

Meanwhile, heat oil in a large skillet over medium-low heat. Add onion; cook until soft and translucent, about 5 minutes. Raise heat to medium-high and add garlic, zucchini, carrots, thyme, and red pepper flakes.

Sauté, stirring frequently, until vegetables are tender and golden around the edges, 8 to 10 minutes. Season with 1/4 tsp. each salt and black pepper. In a large bowl, mix together quinoa, vegetables, and fresh chives and serve.

**FRIDAY** (No waste – check left overs first)
Breakfast

## FRENCH TOAST w/ A TWIST (NO-BREAD OATMEAL)
BASE

- 2 1/4 cup water
- 1 1/2 cup oats
- 1/4 teaspoon sea salt

Bring the water to a boil in a saucepan. Add the salt and oats. Cook, uncovered, until the oats are done and the water has completely evaporated.

Pour the cooked oatmeal into an oiled 8 x 8 baking dish.

FILLING
- ½ Cup applesauce/2 eggs
- 2/3 cup coconut milk
- 1 Tablespoon maple syrup
- dash of salt
- 1/2 teaspoon organic vanilla extract
- ½ teaspoon. cinnamon
- a few scrapes of nutmeg

Mix the filling ingredients well. I usually make both components the night before and assemble everything in the morning.

In the morning, preheat oven to 375 degrees. Pour the filling mix into a pie plate. Cut the chilled oatmeal into nine equal squares. Dip oatmeal squares into mixture, allow to soak for 30 seconds on each side.

Over medium-low heat, melt 1 tablespoon of butter or coconut oil in a non-stick pan. Place 2 slices of oatmeal 'bread' at a time into the pan and cook until golden brown, approximately 2 to 3 minutes per side. Remove from pan and place on baking sheet in oven for 5-10 minutes. Repeat with all 9 slices. Serve immediately with maple syrup or your favorite topping.

Lunch

## QUINOA BURRITO BOWL
Yields: 1-2 servings

- ¾ cup cooked quinoa, cooled
- ¼ cup BPA free can black beans, rinsed and drained
- ¼ cup corn, thawed if frozen
- 2 tomatoes, chopped
- 2 pinches parsley, finely chopped
- 2 teaspoons olive oil
- ½ avocado, chopped
- Juice of ½ lemon

- ¾ ounce fresh cheddar, finely chopped
- Pinch Cayenne Pepper
- Salt, pepper, garlic powder (optional to taste)

Mix all ingredients in a bowl. Taste, adjust spices and enjoy cold or warm.

*Dinner (next page)*


## HURRY CURRY
Serves: 4

- 2 tsp olive oil
- 1/2 cup chopped white or yellow onion
- 1/2 cup red bell peppers, sliced thinly
- 1 small jalapeño pepper (1/4 tsp), sliced
- 2 cloves garlic, minced
- 2 teaspoon ground cumin
- 1 teaspoon ground coriander
- 1 tablespoon curry powder
- 2 tsp raw organic cane sugar (this small amount of sugar helps make this dish successful with a balance of sweet, and mildly spicy.)
- 1 pound African yams (found at International store)
- 1 cup sugar snap peas
- 1 cup light coconut milk from a can, (freeze in a ziplock bag the rest for another time if you wish)
- 1 tablespoons cornstarch
- 1 tablespoons water
- 2 tablespoons chopped fresh cilantro (optional if you don't have it)
- sea salt to taste

Heat oil in large, nonstick saucepan over medium heat. Sauté onion, red pepper, and jalapeño until vegetables begin to soften, about 3 minutes. Add garlic, sauté for 30 seconds more.

While gently stirring, season with cumin, coriander, and curry powder. Cook for 1 minute. Stir in coconut milk, sugar, and sugar snap peas. Bring to a boil. Reduce heat, and simmer, uncovered for 2 minutes.
Stir in yams, and increase heat to medium-high. Cook and stir until shrimp is cooked through, about 4 minutes.

In a small bowl, combine cornstarch with 1 tablespoon of water. Stir into shrimp mixture, and cook until sauce has thickened, about 1 minute. Add salt to taste. Remove from heat, serve. Sprinkle chopped cilantro on individual servings with white rice.

## SATURDAY
Brunch

## BEAN REAL LOAF
Serves: 6

Dried red peas are best soaked overnight, or for several hours.

- ½ pound dried kidney beans (1 full cup)
- 1 medium onion, finely chopped
- 1 medium carrot, peeled and thinly sliced (helps combat gas)
- 1 Tablespoon garlic, minced
- 2 Tablespoons fresh parsley, finely chopped
- 1 Tablespoon of favorite barbeque sauce (see BOSS sauce)
- 1 teaspoon coriander
- ¾ teaspoon cumin
- ½ teaspoon sea salt Pepper to taste
- 2 Tablespoons flour
- ½ cup coconut milk (prefer full cream from BPA-free can-use remainder from Friday)

Boil or cook red peas (kidney beans) until tender.
Preheat oven to 350 F degrees. Combine cooked red peas, onion, garlic, parsley, coriander, carrot, cumin, salt, and pepper in a medium bowl.
Add flour and combine well, making sure to mix all ingredients together. You can also combine the ingredients in a food processor. Add the coconut milk last to make a batter.
Pour the mixture in an oiled (5 cup) loaf pan. Bake at 350 F degrees for 30-35 minutes or until the loaf is golden brown.

## POP CHOY
Serves: 6

- 1 lb Bok Choi
- 2 Tablespoons of Coconut Oil
- 1 Large Yellow Onion, diced
- 2 Plum/Roma tomatoes, diced
- 2 teaspoons sea salt
- 1 Teaspoon black Pepper
- 2 Cloves Garlic, minced
- 1 Tablespoon Ginger, thinly sliced
- 2 sprigs of fresh Thyme

Cut Bok choy stem at very end near root area. Wash bok choy to remove the dirt, chop into 1/8" (estimated) pieces.

In a medium non-stick skillet, sauté the onions, tomatoes, and garlic together in the coconut oil.

Add bok choy to the ingredients in the pot, and then add about 2 tablespoons of water. Add salt and black pepper. Cover the pot and let the bok choy steam until soft. Taste the stew; it should have a taste like it is ready, now add the ginger and thyme.

Turn the fire to low and let it simmer some more for about 3 minutes. Serve with white rice.

Dinner

## SPICY SHELLS & CROWNS
Serves: 2-4

- Coarse sea salt and ground pepper
- 12 ounces short pasta
- 2 tablespoons olive oil + 1 teaspoon to boil pasta
- 2 garlic cloves, thinly sliced
- 1/2 teaspoon red-pepper flakes

- 1 head broccoli (about 1 pound), cut into bite-size florets, stalks peeled and thinly sliced
- 1/2 cup grated Parmesan

In a large pot of boiling salted water, cook pasta, adding 1 teaspoon of olive oil until al dente. Reserve 1/2 cup pasta water; drain pasta and return to pot.

While pasta is cooking, heat oil in a large skillet over medium, add garlic and red-pepper flakes; cook, stirring occasionally, until garlic is golden, 1 to 2 minutes. Add broccoli and 1/2 cup water; season with salt and pepper. Cover and cook until broccoli begins to soften, about 8 minutes. Uncover and continue to cook until water has evaporated and broccoli is crisp-tender, 1 to 2 minutes more.

Transfer pasta in pot, add broccoli mixture, Parmesan (reserve some for later), and enough pasta water to create a thin sauce that coats pasta. Serve sprinkled with remaining Parmesan.

# THE FLAVOR OF FAVOR: SWEET & SOUR

You need to be what you want to attract. Love is a verb, not a noun. Love does; it is choice. When you do nothing, you are still making a choice. It could be that you are focusing too much on whether you are in love (noun) and not making enough of an effort to love (verb) your partner. There's an aspect of love that's a choice, so you need to both. Most of us forget the verb can create the noun and the noun most times inspires the verb.

Many people second guess and go over a dozen different lists wondering if they get it right. I meet with countless entrepreneurs, and talk with many wealthy guys, about marketing plans and fundraising, and there were times where I could have contemplated on whether or not these men could have been a good choice for me. My husband sees plenty of women, more attractive than me, and as an African American man; the numbers are in *his* favor. However, we both have to wake up every day *knowing* that we have a blessing. Long- term compatibility is about sharing common values, respect and building something together. It's not about combing through someone's imperfections.

You really want to find the perfect partner-not the perfect person. It's not about lowering your standards- it's about having reasonable expectations and knowing what is important as you grow in maturity.

If you're always looking at what someone isn't, you will never be satisfied. It's natural, while dating, to look over the person we are dating through a behavioral lens, but view ourselves based on our intentions. This is why people usually attribute what's lacking in a relationship to their partner. We need to keep in mind that perception goes both ways. For instance, if we had planned a date and then learned your boss is expecting you to do a presentation after little notice, you may have a tendency to keep looking at the time and feel it is justifiable. The person you are with may have no idea of your situation and only sees that you are inconsiderate and inattentive.

Take the approach to look at each other's good qualities, rather than looking at the flaws, because we all have flaws. I have a girlfriend who pokes at me regarding my lack of reality show and television drama updates. I love to see strong women on the big screen and on TV. However, I find the line between women being strong and women who are self-centered can be blurry.

"He should think I am the most beautiful woman he has ever seen in his life, if not then we should just cut our losses right now," Yolanda raved.

"Well, I would hope he sees more in you than your beauty, because what happens when that fades?" I responded.

I stopped and remembered to whom I was speaking. This is the girlfriend who barely gets a good night sleep if she is spending the night with a date, because she will wake up at the crack of dawn to wash her face and reapply make-up before her date awakes. You are setting yourself up to be lied to if you think any man thinks the woman he is with is the most beautiful person he has seen in his *life* and vice versa. I want to be fawned over like the next woman, but I also believe I bring a package to the relationship. Shows with titles of Housewives, that are actually jump offs and love that isn't accompanied by any tenderness, is precisely why the only reality about most of these otherwise attractive women is that they have a lot of everything, *but* a man.

"Do you really think there are many women who confuse strength for self-absorption?" My friend Yvonne asked me. I couldn't utter a word, before she went on to describe a guy who would cook for her and send her sweet texts throughout her day.

"He listens to the trials of my day to day and asked me lots of questions about what I wanted in the future, what my family life was like which, in my experience, guys are not good about doing. He opens doors for me and responded to my texts in a reasonable amount of time. He seeks out great events for us to go to, and told me I was all he was looking for. What girl doesn't want to hear that?"

"But", she continued, "At the same time, he just seemed quirky. His house only had pictures of Marvel comic prints His clothing reminds me of Garanimals for grown-ups, and there are video games and controllers strewn all over his coffee table. It's like walking into a dorm room. He isn't in a fraternity.

He doesn't go to the gym. None of those things seem to fit my idea of someone with whom I'd want to build a life. Am I one of *those* women?"

In reflection, I think many of us have been more critical of someone else's quirks than our own at some point. Yvonne admitted that she hadn't stopped long enough to be aware of how her sense of power affected her relationships. "I would see I wasn't getting what I wanted, and we all hear how the sparks eventually dim, so I want to start out with fireworks. If I don't see them right off, and I don't feel I am getting what I want, I break up with a guy."

Another girlfriend at our table, Kim, chimed in, "I felt the same way, but when I met my husband, I realized, that if I went in with an attitude of expecting things from him, instead of being appreciative for who he was, I would be sabotaging myself. I made a decision to see what he brought to the relationship, rather than what he didn't. After all, there were some things I wasn't bringing to the relationship."

One friend I spoke with said that she broke up with a boyfriend because he didn't praise at church the way she expected. He also didn't call enough during the day. Never mind that he was an attorney, who spent days in the court room and had shared with her that he believed in Matthew 6:6 from the Bible: "But when you pray, go into your room and shut the door and pray to your Father who is in secret." She wanted someone who was more available, and strongly anointed. It was amusing, because she thought it was a problem that he needed to change. It never occurred to this 'church girl', that she may need to become a tad more understanding.

I was working with one of my business partners the other day, discussing some of our customers, and she shared a story about her latest date from the previous weekend. After listening to the scenario, I remember seeing a bit of my previous self in her reaction. So, I tried to bring both discussions into context, by describing the two kinds of daters: magnifiers and gratifiers. She sounded like a magnifier, which was the very thing that was frustrating her about her customers. I tried to explain the difference in the two like this: Say you have a customer looking to buy a blouse. She tells you she needs it to go with a particular suit. She would like the cut to be fitted, stylish, French cuffs, and in a particular price range. A gratifier will take her measurements, go onto your website www.k2wcustom.alfadesigner.com (shameless plug), create a blouse to her own criteria, put it in the cart, and buy.

She is done, it only took minutes. You get paid. Isn't this the ideal customer?

191

A magnifier, on the other hand, goes onto the same site, designs a blouse to her specific criteria, and thinks, "This blouse is cool, but maybe I should look at something in that boutique down the street for something that *could be* better. Maybe I can go to Nordstrom Rack and find something on sale." So the magnifier gets up, changes her clothes, gets in her car and travels to a store to look for something off the rack.

Now, it would be fair to assume that the magnifier may end up with a great blouse-after all she can touch them and the brands have been tested, in order to make it into the store, but that doesn't necessarily make it better for her. A gratifier isn't looking for a name to signify quality, although she does have high standards.

She wants something tailored to her, custom to her own perfect imperfections, and when she's found it, she doesn't wonder if she will find something more stylish at another store. She is aware that designer names say more about what people see on the outside than what they see on the inside. She had a particular price range, she found it and she saved travel and time, so she doesn't feel like there is a better value somewhere else. She wanted a flattering fit and she's tailored it for her own unique curves, so she doesn't wonder if she can find something more flattering at a boutique that carries limiting sizes.

A magnifier, on the other hand, believes she has her own unique style, but only when it has someone else's name on it. She will celebrate her full figure by spending money on a designer that only makes handbags, not clothes in her size. She will spend another four hours or even four days looking for the perfect blouse, even though she may not find anything better, leaving her to go back home and buy the blouse she originally designed. (If the design is still on her lap top, which by now, she didn't save on her computer, has to reboot and start over again.)

If the magnifier does find a slightly cuter blouse, on sale, do you think she will be any happier than the gratifier is with hers?

The odds aren't likely. While the gratifier is content knowing she has something great that's on its way, a magnifier will always be looking closer, deeper and longer, on a quest to be sure she has perfection. And we know that we can never travel far enough or long enough to meet everyman and if we did- no man is perfect. The entire process can create anxiety.

Meanwhile, think of all the time and energy wasted on making this decision, all for ten dollars cheaper and less than ten percent cuter. Since you took so long to make your decision, you put undue pressure on yourself to make sure it's just right. It's like women who say, "I've done well so far on my own. I've waited this long for Mr. Right, I am not about to settle now." No one wants to have gone through the entire struggle only to end up with a 'good enough' blouse, that may not garner any compliments, or a 'good enough' guy, just like to one you met and left for someone with a higher title years earlier. In summary, you should buy the blouse with possibilities or date the guy with possibilities, the first time around, knowing that if YOU are factored into the equation, you make everything better. After all, you aren't the issue-or could *not* making a choice say more about you than what you are choosing?

I realize that a blouse isn't like a relationship, but whether it's a blouse or a relationship, gratifiers tend to be happier in life that magnifiers. Gratifiers can be present and articulate what they want. They can identify their deal breakers and they can make a choice, even if there's no guarantee that it's perfect. Magnifiers want to keep looking for someone better and if they do test something out, they do so with an attitude of looking for something wrong or wondering if they are settling. They will spend years dating someone, not sure if he is the right person to marry. It won't be because she isn't sure how she feels about this person. It's that she's not sure if there isn't someone better out there. They don't understand that not getting 100 percent of what we want isn't just acceptable-it's normal.

So, they remain in the cycle, wondering, *"Is this the best I can do?"* There is regret before you actually make a decision. The longer it takes to make a decision, the more likely you are to focus on the faults and nobody will ever seem to measure up. You may have one guy who seems fabulous, but compare him to another guy who makes more money, but has no time for you, and both choices start to look less appealing. The first guy seems less driven; the second guy seems less romantic or emotionally available.

It's simple to choose between 'pretty good' catch and 'completely wrong'; however you get wrecked with anxiety while trying to choose between two pretty goods, which start to look like two 'just alrights.'

Bring any new person into the mix and they may temporarily look like a better option. However, you should keep in mind that if you look hard enough or long enough, you are bound to find something wrong. You could trade your seven for a nine, but eventually you could run into a rough patch that pushes their number down, and you will eventually trade the nine in for another seven.

The gratifiers rarely end up with a blouse of less value than they should have; nor do they pick a guy who's less of an option than what they should have. They're happy because they know that good enough is definitely good enough and anyone who would say otherwise may have on a designer shirt, but if you look close enough, it itches like crazy. They realize that nothing in life is perfect- not friends, not blouses, not celebrities, not designers, not meals, not spouses- so taking a great option, and appreciating it for *all* of what it is, makes sense.

If you didn't start your relationship with the lifestyle that works best for you, you're not stuck. Almost all of the couples I talked to, at one point, thought they would always be in the careers that were making their lives miserable and putting pressure on their bond together. Get rid of some stress in your life and your relationship by abandoning other people's ideas of how your relationship should look. Sometimes together, sometimes at different moments, couples questioned whether they were where they wanted to be, rather than where they needed to be, and simply asking the questions to each other led to changes that have made them healthier, less stressed and happier with each other.

Describe your dream marriage to each other, while you are getting to know each other. There may be things your partner wants of which you are not aware, or about which you have strong feelings. There may also be desires, of your own, that you think you've made known but haven't actually communicated all that clearly.

Talking about a shared future also helps reinvigorate the relationship with that element that often goes missing in periods when you're feeling bored or less connected; it gives you a sense of possibility.

When Shannon, a single mom, and her boo left their corporate jobs to start a business together, she said that some acquaintances and coworkers volunteered commentary on the choices she and her now husband made. They said things such as, "What if he leaves you? Oh my God, how can you pay the tuition for your children's private schooling? Don't you feel like you should be making more money?" Her response was, "We're just happier. Deal with that. These choices weren't easy, but this is what we want."

It is critical in the relationship cycle to have interest in each other. As a date you are curious and as a couple it helps you grow together. Healthy couples remain curious about each other's experiences and inner lives, such as their thoughts, feelings, and dreams.

A great way to cultivate your connection is to talk about the parts of you that not everyone sees — because good communication goes beyond talk of tasks, what's for dinner, errands and kids. (Those topics, of course, also are important. But so is delving into the intimate and often overlooked conversations.)

What are you looking forward to this week, this month, this year?

Would you diet or would you work out?

What do you wear to bed?

What are your favorite books?

If you had a favorite character in a book or movie who would you be & why?

What's your favorite music you're listening to these days?

What's your favorite vacation idea?

Describe the perfect you day (or if you could do anything you wanted for a day, what would it be?)

Are you an animal lover or would you avoid keeping animals at home?

What kind of entertainment do you like?

Backpacking or a luxury hotel?

Are you a morning person?

How do you feel/experience love best?

What comes to your mind when you think of your exes?

What's your idea of romance?

Would you like to live in the countryside or in a metropolitan area?

I would be in a better place if…?

What do you do over the weekends?

If I spent a typical day in your shoes, describe what I would experience?

Where do you get your news?

What are your favorite apps that you use often?

What do you have for breakfast?

What's an absolute no-no in a relationship?

What do you need from (me) where we are right now?

How do you express conflict?

What is the best thing that has ever happened to you?

# *Mo' BETTA' SUBSTITUTES*

**Agave for sugar:**

- Honey: Replace with equal amounts.

- Maple Syrup: Replace with equal amounts.

- Brown Rice Syrup: Use half as much agave+ (up to) 1/2 cup liquid

- Corn Syrup: Use half as much agave+ (up to) 1/3 cup liquid

- White Sugar: For every 1cup sugar called for use 2/3 cup agave minus 1/4 cup liquid.

- Brown Sugar: For every 1cup sugar called *for*, use 2/3 cup agave minus 2 tablespoons liquid.

Agave nectar contains more calories than sugar (20 calories per teaspoon compared to 15 calories in sugar) and is 90% fructose. However, since agave is significantly sweeter than sugar, less is needed when used for substituting. Unlike other sweeteners, agave contains iron, calcium, potassium and magnesium. Due to naturally occurring steroids, *agave is not considered safe for pregnant women.*

Individuals trying to lose weight may want to choose a non-caloric, like Coconut Nectar or Crystals (Coconut Secrets Brand) Stevia sweetener instead.

**Stevia for Sugar**: 1Tablespoon of Sugar=teaspoon of Stevia, 2 cups of sugar= 3-4 tablespoons of Stevia

**Vanilla for sugar**: Cutting sugar in half and adding a teaspoon of vanilla as a replacement can give just as much flavor with significantly fewer calories. You can't sub this one in equal ratios, but if you're baking, try cutting 2 tablespoons of sugar and adding an extra 1/2 teaspoon of vanilla extract.

**Nonfat Greek Yogurt for Mayo or Sour Cream**: Next time a recipe calls for either of those fattening ingredients, try using the yogurt instead. You may want to play around with spices and seasonings, but by making the swap, you can cut the fat while adding an extra punch of protein.

**Pureed Potato for Cream to Thicken Soup**: Instead of thickening your soups with cream, add pureed sweet potato instead. Not only are you getting less fat, but the potassium in sweet potatoes will help lower blood pressure and reduce your risk of stroke.

**Mashed Avocado for Butter or Oil in Baking**: Some fats are actually good for your body; the fats found in avocados are an example. Like olive oil and nuts, avocados are high in monounsaturated "good" fats, which help you maintain healthy cholesterol levels and stave off heart problems. In contrast, solid fats like butter are high in saturated fats, which raise your cholesterol levels and the risk of cardiovascular disease.

**Mashed Bananas for Sugar, Butter and Fats**: if you're using mashed bananas as a sugar substitute, cut down on the moisture in your recipe by using less milk or water. This will help your baked goods come out with the right texture and firmness. Bananas are high in potassium, which helps lower blood pressure, and they also help keep your digestive system in check.

**Banana ice cream for ice cream**: There's no milk, no cream, no sugar and it has the same, delicious consistency. Freeze bananas, then puree.

**Applesauce for Oil, Butter or Sugar**: They add sweetness to recipes, but it does so with significantly fewer calories than sugar. And without butter, you're cutting the saturated-fat content of baked goods like muffins and breads.

**Rolled Oats for Bread Crumbs**: Oats are high in fiber and healthy carbohydrates. They're packed with nutrients like B vitamins, iron and fiber.

**Zucchini Ribbons or Spaghetti Squash for Pasta**: Use a vegetable peeler or a mandolin to make long, thin noodle-like slices of zucchini or spaghetti squash. Skip the boiling and simply bake or sauté the "noodles" for a few minutes. It's an easy way to cut the calories in your favorite pasta meals and sneak more vegetables into your dinner.

**Black beans for flour**: Swapping out flour for a can of black beans (drained and rinsed, of course) in brownies is a great way to cut out the gluten and fit in an extra dose of protein, Plus, they taste great. When baking, swap out 1 cup flour for 1 cup (15oz can)black bean puree.

**Almond flour for wheat flour**: This gluten-free switch gives any baked good a dose of protein, omega-3s, and a delicious nutty flavor. If you're substituting in your recipe, remember to increase the amount of rising agent (by about 1/2 teaspoon per cup of almond flour added) to account for the extra weight.

**Marshmallow Fluff for frosting**: By replacing the fat and sugar in frosting with marshmallow, you achieve the perfect consistency with many fewer calories. While two tablespoons of marshmallow has just 40 calories and 6 grams of sugar (and no fat!), the same amount of conventional frosting can pack up to 100 calories, 14 grams of sugar, and 5 grams of fat.

**Flax meal or chia seeds for eggs**: Mix 1 tablespoon ground flax meal with 3 tablespoons of warm water and whisk with a fork to combine. Let it sit in the fridge for 5-10 minutes before subbing for 1 egg in any baked recipe. Chia-1 tablespoon chia seeds with 1 cup of water left to sit for 15 minutes yields a perfect 1-to-1 egg substitute.

**Grated steamed cauliflower for rice**: You will cut both calories and carbs with this simple switch. The texture is virtually the same, as is the taste.

**Coconut Aminos for Soy sauce**:  a soy, nut, dairy, gluten, everything free, raw, vegan liquid sauce can be substituted anywhere you would use soy or fish sauce. Although it's not cheap, it tastes like a sweet soy sauce & is made from fermented sap of the coconut tree.

## Got Milk? *Not Milk?*

### Coconut Milk

If you like the taste of coconut or are into the coconut water health craze, then you'll definitely enjoy coconut milk. This watery milk can be used in various dishes and comes packed with potassium and saturated fats — fats that are great for you because they contain lauric and capric acid that offer antiviral and antifungal properties. Rich and creamy, So Delicious Coconut Milk is great in cooking and baking, and it's my preferred dairy-free milk substitute when I want to drink it straight from the glass.

### Rice Milk

Rice milk is not as thick as soy or dairy milks, and has a somewhat translucent consistency. Because it is slightly sweet, rice milk works well in dessert recipes and is not suited for savory or salty dishes, such as mashed potatoes. Compared to soy and almond milk, rice milk has less protein.

### Almond Milk

Milk made from almonds or other nuts, such as cashew milk has a creamy consistency similar to soy milk and a nutty taste perfect for making vegan fruit smoothies or other creamy drinks and desserts, though they don't taste much like dairy milk, and are best in non-savory dishes. Be sure to shake your almond milk well before using. If you can't find almond milk at your grocery store, try making a homemade almond milk or cashew milk.

### Soy Milk

The good news is soy milk is healthy, cheap, and easy to find and use. The bad news is...if there is any; soy products have been found to contain small doses of isoflavones, which are chemically similar to estrogens, this could be bad or good, depending on your own personal family history. From a nutritional perspective, soy milk has almost as much protein as dairy milk, less fat, no cholesterol, and, since most soy milks are fortified, is a comparable source of calcium. Vegans should make sure to find a brand that is fortified with Vitamin B12. Soy milk is an excellent dairy substitute for baking or for kids.

**Gluten to Gluten-Free**

The below are safe substitutes to replace wheat, rye, barley, and oat as ingredients in recipes and food selections; can be in the form of flour and starch for use in baking and cooking. Replacing wheat flour with a gluten-free substitute is not nearly so simple or straightforward as I would like. No other flour can singlehandedly duplicate all the characteristics we love in wheat, but blending several different flours together can get mighty close. I think buying a pre-blended mix is a good way to go if you're just starting out or bake infrequently. In the past, I've done all my gluten-free baking with the all-purpose mix. It's a blend of white and brown rice flours, tapioca starch, and potato starch, and I think it does an excellent job in smaller baked goods like cookies, scones, muffins, and quick breads.

*Try*

**Grain flours/starches**: Rice, Corn, Sorghum

**Legume flours**: Soy, Chickpeas, Fava Bean, Peanut, Black Bean

**Seed Flours**: Flax seed, Millet, Buckwheat, Quinoa

**Starches**: Potato, Tapioca, Arrowroot, Sweet Potato

**Nut Flours**: Almond, Walnut, Filbert

# THE HONEY & THE MONEY

You aren't going *to* be happy in a paycheck competition. Regardless of the amount of money you or the one you are with are making. Each of you has a desire to be appreciated. You need to ask yourself if the success you achieve outside of the home is worth losing what you have inside of your home. You also need to consider whether or not that person is providing for you or investing in you.

Does he show his love publicly? Does he respect you and not stand for anyone, not even his mother, disrespecting you? Will he provide for you, even when things are tight for him?

The provision always leads to great debates with men and women, but you need to have good communication in your relationship. If you start out wining and dining just to impress someone, when you should probably be offering to cook meals at home or take her to a restaurant you can afford, then you shouldn't be upset if she has expectations of getting money from you.

In the same mode of thinking, if you start out dressing leaving nothing to the imagination and you give up the goodies before the appetizer arrives, you shouldn't be upset if he has expectations of only getting the panties. I agree that if you have urges and you want to act on them, that is clearly your choice. However, you need to understand *who* you are, and whether you will be alright if the other person doesn't have the same expectations in the relationship as you do. Men don't mind being needed. They also appreciate hearing the qualities you appreciate in them.

It is great to set goals for yourselves, but you should never approach it like you are in a paycheck competition. You are going to see that your needs are going to change depending on where you are in your life. The most important thing is to have discussion about each of your needs. There has been much discussion about leaning in and not enough consideration on what you're leaning on. Is your success outside of the home worth losing what you have inside of the home? Which is more important-someone providing for you or investing in you?

Seeking support, feeling close, forming strong emotional bonds, and expressing feelings are essential to a fulfilled life. Many studies have shown that having these experiences helps support our physical and psychological well-being.

Do you remember spending hours on the phone talking to your true love, conversations at the dinner table with family and weekends hanging at the mall or out at the park playing sports with your friends? In the recent age of electronic, instant messages, video games and reality TV, people have raised their expectations of intimacy but lowered the meaning on who you should be getting it from and who is responsible for getting it. "We are communicating less with our other circles of influence and expecting to get it all from those with whom we are coupled," reflected Yvonne.

"The media, along with the women's independence movement, has put out so many negative images on male social activity, that you risk being tagged a dog if you have more than one confidante- and that one better be your girl!" exclaimed Damon.

A smaller social circle makes men touchy to a female's emotions—especially their negative emotions. That's not to say that wives are not reactive to men's feelings, but having a wider social network allows women more opportunities to calibrate their emotional lives.

For a long time, the prevalent definition of closeness in a relationship has revolved around the sharing of feelings and insecurities. Although this is essential, it can also be too narrow to support the roots necessary for each participant's growth. Without strong roots, a relationship will wither. When a person feels their partner supports their growth, they have feelings of freedom, which allows them to surrender inhibitions. This fuels, not only the expansion of love, but the sexual desire and eroticism increasingly expected, if relationships are to satisfy for a lifetime.

We sat together, discussing this issue, when Beyoncé's song *Blow* rang across the airwaves. Then, we began chatting about her incarnation of empowerment and being sexual, on her own terms. We all agreed the entertainment industry often demands the sexualization of women, as a precursor for their success. So, we put all of our critiques aside against gratuitous sexualization. This isn't generalizing the concern that girls internalize the notion that their worth is intrinsically tied to their bodies, and the desirability of those bodies, but to use this as an example to have dialog about a woman coming into her own choices, while being the wife of a man in the spotlight.

People can see from her style and her career, that Beyoncé owns her feminism. She shapes it to fit her strengths, weaknesses, and dreams, in order to better herself and express her thoughts on what it means to be a successful woman in 2014, living in the spotlight of opinions that believe women should settle in roles rather than chase goals. I believe a woman experiences feminism when she owns all parts of herself.

"You can't experience real intimacy until both people are comfortable in their own skin. That is what I heard in the music. Some of her critics still see her as Beyoncé, singing independent national anthems for girls, but her latest work is about being MRS. Carter. She is a wife who can show that she is in a space, where she has just as much at the table as her husband does," says Kaneeka. "Both she and Jay Z seem to have equal power in defining what they want and what they really think and believe. The two of them have their own sense of self-assurance and vulnerability into the relationship," she continued.

"If you truly believe you can't survive without a relationship, you don't have power to really be yourself within a relationship," responded Yvonne.

There are power plays too often in relationships, where one partner gives up too much of themselves. The priorities and standards of one person, often take a back seat behind relationship pressures; one person will make the other's goals more of a priority and tends to concede on big decisions. "Yeah, I remember my mom doing it, and her mom before her, and I watched as they both grew resentful," I retorted.

"Now, many more women are going into a relationship trying to set the tone and act on our own behalf, but men see it as disagreeable," Yvonne said.

"I see it both ways, especially now that women are more economically independent," Karl chimed in. "But you have to be confident that it will be reciprocated or one person will be in a position in which all they do is accommodate, with no appreciation until they don't have any more to give. Then, they bail, rather than feeling like a doormat."

"It's really about awareness of your partner's emotions. In order to be fulfilled, each person has to have enough power to recognize the affect their partners emotions have on them," explained Pam. "You feel appreciated when your partner responds to how something makes you feel."

A relationship is rarely equal, but it has to feel fair. That requires flexibility and sensitivity. People feel like a priority when they see you give attention to their needs. Occasionally in marriage, or when couples are cohabitating, flexibility is guised under the mirage of division of labor or paying bills. However, the lines get cloudy when determining when the decisions one person makes could have an effect on the couple.

"Respect should apply to both people in a relationship. Respect doesn't mean one person always gets their way. It means I recognize that you are worthy of getting the same accommodations you would like me to give you," Pam added.

No one should keep lists as to who conceded or who got whose way last, in order to measure how fair they are being treated. People can accept unequal division of labor, but they still want to be appreciated. They want to be able to make decisions, according to life changes, and are not taken for granted.

It's easy for someone to fail to see where they are being selfish, if they were raised with certain male female roles, forgetting the person you are dating has their own unique qualities that are not gender specific. Communication is the key.

Be mindful when you and your partner are caught in a power struggle, where one of you is trying, in vain, to influence the other and you're continually locked in an argument, often about the same issue over and over again. This is usually a sign, some experts believe, that a partner hasn't completely surrendered their *me* for the advancement of *we*.

When you show interest in your partner's needs, it is easier for them to be open in seeing things from your perspective. You get better results when your partner knows they are supported by you, rather than faulted. When both people feel safe being vulnerable in a relationship, you can be confident that each person will give their whole self.

As women, we are hard-wired to be nurturers. This means we have special skills to read the emotions of others as a way to bring comfort, anticipate needs or give direction. Men aren't wired that way, but women still expect that type of 'intuition' from them. We would be better served to recognize how they are wired and communicate our needs.

Women tend to want to talk it out, right then, whereas retreat. Men often display intimacy in unspoken practical acts, which a woman can't often recognize, especially when she feels her emotions are stuck in neutral. Do you want your partner to see you as the kind of person who is mostly right or the right person who mostly kind?

He who tries to dominate in the relationship may win the battle, but they will lose the war. "No one is above anyone in a relationship. Both people are IN it. Constant arguments are negativity, and negativity brings you down. No one wants to feel down. If you are making reference to winning and losing in your relationship, you've already lost. It's not even about being right or wrong if you want to be together, because the one who is constantly made to feel wrong will go somewhere else to get right."

You can't bully someone into loving you. Humans are the only species who can use free will to change course. A goose is hardwired to travel to a warmer climate in the winter, a tree cannot pick up and move when it's depleted the ground of its nutrients- it just stays planted there and dies. You can't use religious or societal examples. The Bible started out with Ten Commandments, the Qur'an several more; but our Legislature has written several million and people still break them every day without second thought.

# *CAKES, SWEETS, THE ULTIMATE COOKIE, GOOD NUTS*

## CANDIED WALNUTS

*Although walnuts are naturally sweet in flavor, they have a bitter skin. This is how I remove the skin. Preheat the oven to 350 F, then spread them on a cookie sheet & toast for 8 minutes, remove from oven & cool. Put walnuts in a sieve and rub against the screen until the skins fall off. Store in the freezer.

- 4 cups of raw walnut halves
- 1/2 cup extra virgin olive oil
- 1/4 cup agave nectar
- 1/2 cup organic raw cane sugar

In a large bowl mix walnuts with olive oil & stir until thoroughly coated. Add the agave nectar & stir until well coated, then add the sugar and still until well coated.

Warm a large cast iron skillet to medium high, add the walnuts and stir consistently for a minute and a half, until all the liquid is gone.

Transfer the walnuts onto wax/parchment paper with a fork, spread out and let cool. -Great snack if you add raisins.

## ALMOND CRANBERRY OATMEAL COOKIES (P)
Serves: 24 cookies

- 1cup All-Purpose flour
- 1teaspoon baking soda
- 1/2 teaspoon salt
- 1/4 teaspoon ground cinnamon
- 1cup almond butter
- 1/2 cup brown sugar
- 1/2 cup Almond milk
- 1teaspoon vanilla extract
- 1cup old fashioned oats
- 1/2 cup dried cranberries
- 1/2 cup vegan chocolate chips (or regular chocolate chips)

Preheat oven to 350 degrees F. Line a large baking sheet with parchment paper or spray with coconut oil and set aside.

In a medium bowl, whisk together flour, baking soda, salt, and cinnamon. Set aside.

With an electric fitted with a paddle attachment, combine the almond butter and brown sugar. Mix until light and fluffy, about 2-3 minutes. Mix in the almond milk and vanilla extract, scraping down the sides if necessary.

Turn the mixer to low and add the dry ingredients. Mix until just combined. Stir in the oats, dried cranberries, and chocolate chips.

Roll cookie dough into small balls and place on prepared baking sheet, about 2 inches apart. Gently flatten the dough balls with the palm of your hand. Bake cookies for 10 minutes or until they are golden brown around the edges. Let the cookies cool on the baking sheet for 2 minutes. Transfer to a wire cooling rack and cool completely.

## CARAMEL CAKE

- 8 tablespoons of (1stick) of butter
- 1 cups of cane sugar*  For every 1cup sugar called for use 2/3 cup agave minus 1/4 cup liquid.
- 1cup Caramel Syrup (see next)
- 2 cups sifted all-purpose flour
- 2 teaspoons baking powder
- ½ teaspoon salt
- 1cup milk (if added agave, minus cup milk)
- 2 large eggs

Preheat oven to 375 F. Spray two 8-inch layer cake pans with coconut oil or line with wax paper.

In a large mixing bowl, beat butter, add 1cup of sugar (agave) gradually, until light & fluffy.

In a medium mixing bowl, sift flour, baking powder, and salt together. Add sifted ingredients to creamed mixture, alternating with milk.

In a separate mixing bowl, beat eggs for about 3 minutes, until foamy. (cold metal bowls in freezer help foam) Add remaining sugar, and beat until there is fine foam. Stir into cake batter until blended.

Divide batter between two cake pans. Bake for about 25 minutes. Remove pans from oven. Check cake with toothpick. If toothpick is clean-cake is done. Let cakes cool to room temperature before frosting.

Assembling: Center one cooled cake layer on cake plate. Cover top and sides with generous helping of frosting. Place second layer evenly on frosted layer. Cover with frosting. Cool in refrigerator until ready to serve.

## CARAMEL SYRUP

- 1cup cane sugar*  For every 1cup sugar called for use 2/3 cup agave minus 1/4 cup liquid
- 1cup boiling water

Heat sugar/agave in a heavy skillet over low heat, stir constantly until melted to a brown liquid.  When it bubbles over entire surface, remove from heat. Slowly add boiling water, stirring constantly.  Pour into glass jar or container and cool.


## CARAMEL FROSTING

- 6 tablespoons (3/4 stick) butter
- One 8 ounce package of confectioner's sugar
- 4 tablespoons of heavy cream
- 1teaspoons pure vanilla extract
- Pinch of sea salt

Brown the butter in a heavy pot over medium heat-stir slowly to prevent any burning. Allow butter to cool. In a large mixing bowl, add confectioners' sugar, cream, vanilla extract and salt to the butter, and beat until consistency is smooth.  If frosting is too stiff to spread, add tablespoon of almond milk or cream to thin.


## **COCONUT  PIE CRUST**
Makes 1crust

- 1/ 2 cup whole wheat pastry flour
- cup all-purpose flour (+flour for dusting surface of counter)
- teaspoon baking powder
- 2 teaspoons raw cane sugar
- 1/2 teaspoon sea salt
- 7 tablespoons of solidified coconut oil
- 1teaspoon apple cider vinegar
- ¼  to ½ cup ice water (keep chilled)

Combine flours, baking powder, sugar and salt in a bowl and whisk to mix. Add the coconut oil into the bowl and rub into the flour mixture using your fingers until the mixture resembles small pebbles.

Add the apple cider vinegar to the ice water. Drizzle the water in to the dough a teaspoon at a time, mixing as you add. Stop adding water when the dough holds together as you squeeze in your palm.

Transfer the dough to a clean, floured surface. Shape dough into a ball and then flatten into a disc. Wrap in ziplock bag (squeeze out all air or use Saran wrap) and refrigerate for 45 minutes.

## SWEET POTATO GINGER MAPLE PIE

Makes: 8 servings

- 1 Coconut Pie Crust
- 2 ½ pounds peeled sweet potatoes
- 2 cups of coconut milk
- 1 tablespoons plus 2 teaspoons agar flakes (vegetarian gelatin substitute- made from seaweed, loaded w/ fiber)
- 2 teaspoons fresh ginger, minced
- 1/4 cup pure maple syrup
- 1 teaspoon vanilla extract
- 1 teaspoon of ground cinnamon
- ½ teaspoon grated nutmeg
- 2 tablespoons of arrowroot powder
- 1/2 teaspoon sea salt

Remove pie crust dough and allow it to warm at room temperature

Bake sweet potatoes (375F) until they can be pierced easily with a fork, or dice and cover with water in a large pot covered with water and bring to a rolling boil, until soft-about 30 minutes. Remove from heat and peel/ drain if they are boiled. Measure out 2 cups of the cooked sweet potatoes and set aside.

Unwrap the pie dough and transfer it to a lightly floured surface. Roll dough with a rolling pin into a

12-inch circle and place dough into a pie pan, gently pressing into the bottom and sides. Trim the edges of the crust with a knife and pinch around the top edge to make it decorative.

Preheat the oven to 400F

Wrap the edge of the crust with aluminum foil to prevent it from burning and poke the bottom of the crust several times with a fork. Transfer the crust to the oven and bake for about 6-8 minutes, until golden brown. Remove & set aside.

Lower the temperature of the oven to 375F

In a saucepan over medium heat, bring the coconut milk to a simmer, stirring slowly. Add the agar flakes and the ginger and simmer for about 8 minutes, careful not to boil, stirring often, until agar dissolves. Stir in the maple syrup and vanilla extract and simmer for a minute. Turn off the heat.

Add the sweet potatoes, agar mixture, cinnamon, nutmeg, arrowroot, and the sea salt to a food processor with a metal blade. Blend until creamy and smooth.

Pour the filling into the pie shell and smooth the top with a damp spatula. Bake for 30 minutes, until the filling is warm.

Cool on a wire rack for 2 hours, or until pie has firmed.


## GINGER COCONUT DROPS
Yields: 10 drops

- 4 1/2 cups Water
- 4 cups Brown Sugar
- 4 cups Diced Coconut (flesh from 2 medium coconuts)
- 4 Tablespoons fresh Ginger, minced
- 1 tablespoon Vanilla Flavoring
- 1/4 tsp Sea Salt

Remove flesh from about two medium coconuts and dice into small pieces using small knife

Line a baking sheet with wax paper or greased parchment paper Pour water in large nonstick saucepan add sugar and bring to boil Add coconut, ginger, vanilla, salt and stir

Continue stirring on High heat; the water will reduce and mixture thicken until it bubbles like caramel; continue stirring. Takes about 40 minutes, but worth it!

When it is ready, drop heaps of mixture on baking sheet using large spoon and sit to let cool.

## SWEET & TIPSY COCONUT CAKES
Serves 6-10

- 8 cups of grated or diced fresh coconut meat
- ¾ cup peeled and finely grated ginger
- 1 cup dark rum
- 1 ¼ cups superfine cane sugar

Preheat the oven to 200 F. Using an ovenproof dish, mix the coconut and ginger with a generous amount of the rum. Keep it warm in the oven.

Melt the sugar in a large, heavy-based pan on medium to low heat. When the sugar starts to brown at the edges, stir it with a wooden spoon until smooth. (Watch carefully)

When the sugar is dark brown (like pancake syrup), quickly add the coconut-rum mixture. The timing is important. The mixture may bubble, but stir vigorously until the sugar is well blended with all of the ingredients. Remove from the heat and cool for 20 minutes. Use an ice cream scoop and scoop small balls or moisten your hands and form into small golf ball sizes.

Serve immediately or refrigerate for later.

**CELEBRATION MANGO MOUSSE**:
Serves 4 to6

- 3 to 4 large ripe mangoes
- 1/3 cup superfine sugar
- ¼ cup mango liqueur or other flavored liqueur (such as Grand Marnier or Triple Sec)
- 2 cups heavy cream (or 16 oz. BPA-fee can of coconut cream)
- Mint sprigs; for garnish
- Strawberries; thinly sliced for garnish (optional)

Wash the mangoes, dry with paper towels, and cut them open with a sharp knife. Scoop out all the flesh into a bowl. Process the pulp to a smooth purée in a blender or food processor; do not use a juicer.

Push the mango pulp through a fine-mesh sieve to rid it of any fibers and to keep the pulp smooth. Cover and set aside.

Combine the sugar and liqueur in a cup, and stir together until the sugar mostly dissolves. Add to the mango pulp.

Start whipping the cream, and slowly add the mango pulp as you whip. Continue whipping until the mango and cream are well combined and the mixture is thick, smooth, and creamy. Pour into parfait or other dessert glasses. Chill in the refrigerator, not the freezer, until ready to serve. Garnish with sprigs of mint and strawberries before serving.


**MY MILK SHAKE BRINGS Da Boys to DA YARD** (SOUR SOP PUNCH)

- 1ripe Soursop (Guanabana) *Can be found in international section of grocer in frozen pulp/ Amazon
- 1can Sweetened Condensed Milk 16oz./ Coconut milk (in grocer's fridge) & agave mix
- 1teaspoon grated Nutmeg
- 2 Tablespoons fresh Lime Juice

- 1 tablespoon Vanilla extract
- 5 cups of Water

Add guanabana pulp or peel the guanabana/soursop by hand; put flesh in a large mixing bowl and remove all the seeds.

Put fruit into blender; add 3 cups of water and puree. Pour puree into in the mixing bowl and add 2 to 3 more cups of water. (If you prefer a smooth drink, use a strainer and the additional water to remove fruit fibers.)

Add sweetened condensed milk, nutmeg, lime juice and vanilla and stir to blend

Serve chilled with or without ice cubes. Add a dash of nutmeg to each glass before serving.*Add white rum if you want some zing!

## THIS IS BANANAS WINE
Yields: 24 glasses

- 7 very ripe plantains, peeled and finely sliced
- 5 quarts cold water
- 4 pounds sugar
- 4 1-inch-wide strips soft toast
- 1 tablespoon fresh yeast

In a very large pot, boil the plantains in the water for 20 minutes. Strain and add the sugar to the liquid. Set aside to cool. Spread both sides of each strip of toast with yeast and drop them into the strained liquid.

Lightly cover the jar with a piece of cheesecloth and store in a cool, safe place for 1 week. Strain the liquid after 1 week, and store in an airtight container for 3 weeks. Open and strain for the third time. Store in an airtight container for an additional month.

Finally, open and strain for the fourth and last time, then bottle as wine and cork. You may now chill the wine and serve it as normal; however, the longer it is left, the more mature it will become, so serve it when it suits you. I prefer the total process to take 6 months.

## LEMONGRASS ICED TEA
Yields 5 servings

Lemongrass might help prevent the growth of some bacteria and yeast. Lemongrass also contains substances that are thought to relieve pain, reduce fever, stimulate the uterus and menstrual flow, and have antioxidant properties.

- 4 cups of filtered water
- 1 22-gram package of fresh lemongrass
- ½ cup organic cane sugar (1/2 teaspoon stevia)
- 1 can ginger ale
- 1 lemon wedge for garnish

In a medium saucepan, bring water to a boil. Add lemongrass and continue boiling for 5 minutes.

Remove from heat, cover, and let cool.

Strain and discard lemongrass, then sweeten with sugar/stevia and refrigerate. When ready to serve, pour over ice cubes until glass is half full, then fill remainder with ginger ale. Garnish with a lemon wedge.

## STAMINA STOUT
Yields 3 servings

- 1 bottle of Guinness Stout
- 3 scoops of vanilla ice cream
- ½ teaspoon grated nutmeg
- 1 tsp Jamaican white rum (optional)
- ½ cup hemp milk

- 1 cup almond/coconut milk
- 4 tablespoons condensed milk (or condensed coconut milk-make first, see below)

*Homemade Sweetened Condensed Coconut Milk*
Yields: about 12 ounces

- 1 14 oz. can full-fat coconut milk*
- 1/4 cup honey, or equivalent sweetener of choice

Pour the coconut milk into a small saucepan, and heat over medium-high heat until boiling, about 5 minutes.

Watch your pot closely! Once the coconut milk starts to boil, it can bubble over quickly. Whisk regularly to prevent burning. Reduce the heat, bringing the coconut milk to a simmer, then add the sweetener, whisking until it's completely dissolved.

Allow to simmer for 30 minutes, or until the liquid is reduced by half. Remove from the heat, and allow to cool completely before using in recipes.

*Note: I don't recommend using low-fat or light coconut milk, since those versions are usually just coconut milk that's diluted with water to lower the fat content.

## HOMEMADE CHAI MIX

I add this to my tea, pancakes, and muffins

- 2 tsp ground cinnamon
- 2 tsp ground cardamom
- 1tsp ground coriander
- 1tsp ground ginger
- 1tsp ground cloves
- 1/2 tsp ground white pepper
- pinch Himalayan rock salt

**HGTEA BOMB**  (Honey, Ginger, Tumeric)
Yields: 1/2 cup

- 1/2 cup raw honey (prefereble organic unheated)
- 2-4 tbsp freshly grated ginger (or ground ginger), depending on how strong you prefer
- 2 tsp freshly ground turmeric (or freshly grated turmeric if you can find it)
- 1 organic lemon, freshly grated zest
- 2 pinches ground black pepper

Stir all ingredients together in a bowl. Taste and add more ginger or turmeric if needed. Try to get a strong flavor because you will only add a few teaspoons to a cup of water. Store the HGTea Bomb in a glass jar. Boil a cup of water and let slightly cool (to keep the benefits from the honey intact), stir in a few teaspoons of the honey mixture and drink. You can also add this to your favorite brewed green tea.

### *Coffee (C)*

Coffee has been found to affect a number of neurotransmitters related to mood control, so drinking a morning cup could have an effect on your general sense of wellbeing. Research has also shown that coffee triggers a mechanism in your brain that releases BDNF, which activates your brain stem cells to convert into new neurons, thereby improving your brain health. Interestingly enough, research also suggests that low BDNF levels may play a significant role in depression, and that increasing neurogenesis has an antidepressant effect!

### *Protein (P)*

A high-quality source of protein -like organic eggs, a piece of Gouda cheese or a handful of almonds-helps to keep your blood sugar levels steady for enhanced energy and mood.

### *Bananas*

Bananas contain dopamine, a natural reward chemical that boosts your mood. They're also rich in B vitamins, including vitamin B6, which help to soothe your nervous system, and magnesium, another nutrient associated with positive mood. Please be careful to limit them if you have insulin/leptin resistance

### *Turmeric (Curcumin)* (T)

Curcumin, the pigment that gives the spice turmeric its yellow-orange color, is thought to be the primary component responsible for many of its medicinal effects. Among them, curcumin has neuroprotective properties and may enhance mood and possibly help with depression along with assist in blood circulation.

### *Purple Berries*

Anthocyanins are the pigments that give berries like blueberries and blackberries their deep color. These antioxidants aid your brain in the production of dopamine, a chemical that is critical to coordination, memory function and your mood.

### Animal-Based Omega-3 Fats

Found in fresh organic salmon or supplement form, such as krill oil, the omega-3 fats EPA and DHA play a role in your emotional well-being. Dr. Andrew Stoll, a psych pharmacologist and assistant professor of psychiatry at the Harvard Medical School, found that doses of fish oil did indeed reduce a dramatic 20 percent reduction in anxiety among medical students taking omega-3, while past research has shown omega-3 fats work just as well as antidepressants in preventing the signs of depression, but without any of the side effects.

## MOODY BLUES

*Sugar*

Sugar can lead to fluctuations in blood sugar, which can bring on mood swings, but its role in poor mood actually goes much deeper than that. Entire books have been written on this topic, such as William Duffy's book, *Sugar Blues*. There are at least three potential mechanisms through which refined sugar intake could exert a toxic effect on your mood and mental health:

- Sugar (particularly fructose) and grains contribute to insulin and leptin resistance and impaired signaling, which play a significant role in your mental health

- Sugar suppresses activity of BDNF, which promotes the health of your brain neurons. BDNF levels are critically low in both depression and schizophrenia, which animal models suggest might actually be causative

# INDEX

**A**
Apples, Fried, 172
Apple a Day Sandwich, 161

**B**
Bacon, Fakin, 116
Banana, Fritters, 133 w/fringe, 170
Beans, Drunken Over It, 97
Beans, Black Eyed Pea Fritters, 98
Beans, Black Bean Stew, 103
Beans, Moody Chick Peas, 127
Beans, Sautéed & Zucchini, 111
Beans, Real Loaf, 185
Bison, Meatloaf, Coupled & Tomato Gravy, 160
Bread, Banana Powa Bars, 115
Bread, She'Ra Chia Bread, 121
Bread, Turnin' Heads Snack Bread, 122
Bread, Cranberry Cornbread, 180
Breakfast, Cappuccino Muffins, 128
Breakfast, Dreamy, Creamy Cheese Grits, 147
Breakfast, Porridge, Passion, 129
Breakfast, Porridge, Plantain Power, 130
Breakfast, Banana Fritters, 131
Breakfast, Merry Monday Cakes, 151
Breakfast, Protein Muffin No Fluffin, 154
Breakfast, Eggcelent, 158
Breakfast, Nutter Butter Banana Quesadilla, 163
Breakfast, Hash It Out w/ Legs & Eggs, 167
Breakfast, Hot n Hardy Chick Pea Pancakes, 171
Breakfast, Grown Folks Oats, 175
Breakfast, Scrambled Vegan Eggs, 181
Breakfast, French Toast w/ a Twist, 182
Burger, Red Hot Quinoa, 174

## C

Cake, Caramel Cake, 211
Cakes, Sweet Tipsy Coconut Cakes, 215
Caramel Syrup, 212
Chai Mix, 219
Chicken, Jerk, 71
Chicken, Brown Stew, 73
Chicken, Hot Tweenst the Thighs, 75
Chicken, Rum Coconut, 76
Chicken, Taco Soup, 94
Chicken, No Lie No Fry, 156
Chicken, Ole & Away, 162
Chicken, Pizza Barbeque, 168
Chili, Power Peppered, 106
Coconut, Pie Crust, 212
Coconut, Sweet & Tipsy Cakes, 215
Condiments, Coco Ginger Sauce, 178
Condiments, Ginger Peanut Dipping Sauce, 132
Condiments, Boss Sauce, 59
Condiments, No Yo Mayo, 62 (Vegan)
Condiments, Vegan Ranch, 62
Condiments, Nacho Usual Vegan Cheese, 63
Condiments, Hot N Saucy, 119
Condiments, Blueberry Lime Salsa, 133
Condiments, Jam, Hot Berry, 153
Condiments, Salsa, Chunky, 163
Cookies, Almond Cranberry Oatmeal, 210
Crock Pot, Jambalaya, 91
Crock Pot, Da Yard Beef Stew & Dumplings, 92
Crock Pot, Chicken Taco Soup, 94
Crock Pot, Spinach & Ricotta Lasagna, 95
Crock Pot, Scalloped Potatoes, 96
Crock Pot, Drunken Over It Baked Beans, 97
Crock Pot, Ole & Away, 162
Crock Pot, Chick Peace, 175
Curry, Chick Peas & Curry Run Down, 113
Curry, Hurry, 184

## D

Dessert, Cornmeal & Currant Pudding, 134
Dessert, Sweet Potato Pudding, 135
Dessert, Banana Fritters & Fringe, 170

Dessert, Celebration Mango Mousse, 216
Dessert, My Milk Shake Brings Da Boys to Da Yard, 216
Dips, Nacho Usual Vegan Cheese, 63
Dips, Black Bean Guacamole, 110
Drinks, Lemongrass Iced Tea, 218
Drinks, Stamina Stout, 218
Drinks, This is Bananas Wine, 217
Drinks, Green Goodness, 20
Drinks, HGTea Bomb, 220
Dumplings, Coconut, 92  Simple, 150

**E**
Egg, Protein Muffin No Fluffin, 154

**F**
Fish, Fish Sticks , 31
Fish, Couscous, 32
Fish, Lemony-Ginger, 33
Fish, Tacos, 35
Fish, Ginger Honey Love glazed, 36
Fish, Grits,Wishy Fishy,36
Fish, Grilled Red Snapper, 38
Fish, Cook Whole, 39
Fish, Skillet Fish w/ Garlic & Cilantro, 152

**G**
Gluten, Gluten Free, 201
Grits, Dreamy Creamy Garlic Cheese, 147
Grits, Grit Cakes, 148
Guacamole, Black Bean, 110
Guacamole, Fried, 123

**J**
Jam, Hot Berry, 151

**K**
Kale, Fritters, 112
Kale, What the Kale Salad, 107

**L**
Lentils, 79

List, Pantry, 12
List, Freezer, 14
List, Refrigerator, 14
List, CLEAN & MEAN 2 Week Menu, 144-145

## M

Meatloaf, Bison w/ Tomato Gravy, 162
Meatloaf, Turkey, 77
Menu, 2 week, 147-187
Milk, Not Milk, 200
Muffins, Cappuccino, 128

## N

Noodles, Bayou (Bye You), 78
Noodles, Spicy Sesame, 176
Nuts, Candied Walnuts, 209

## P

Pasta, He's the Mac w/ Cheeze, 108-109
Pasta, Spicy Shells & Crowns, 186
Pizza, Barbeque Chicken, 168
Potato, Baked Sweet Potato Fries, 126
Potato, New, 157
Potato, Onion Flat Bread, 159
Protein, Buckwheat, 80
Protein, Hempseed, 80
Protein, Lentils, 79
Protein, Quinoa, 80
Protein, Soy, 80
Pudding, Cornmeal, 134
Pudding, Sweet Potato, 135

## Q

Questions, 195-196
Quinoa, Chick Burger, 125
Quinoa, Muah!, 182
Quinoa, Power Peppered Chili, 106
Quinoa, Red Hot Quinoa Burger, 174

## R

Rice, It's Your Seasoned, 101

Rice, New Boo Saffron, 105
Rice, Emerald, 153
Rice, Chasing Beans, 166

## S

Salad, Asian Fusion, 155
Salad, Betta Feta, 179
Salad, Broccoli, Sweet & Tangy Chill-out, 133
Salad, Spicy Chick Pea, 61
Salad, Stella's Groove Back, 108
Salad, Sweet Tart Spinach, 173
Salad, What the Kale, 107
Salad, Wild N Out, 131
Salad Dressing, Plantain, 132
Salad Dressing, Ginger Vinaigrette, 156
Salsa, Blueberry Lime, 133
Salsa, Chunky, 163
Sandwiches, Vegan Carrot Dogs, 55
Sandwiches, Vegetarian Couple Hot Dogs, 56
Sandwiches, Can't Get My Fatty Patty, 58
Sandwiches, Do You Feel Me Cheese Steak, 60
Sandwiches, Spicy Chick Pea Salad, 61
Sandwiches, Quinoa Chick Burgers, 129
Sandwiches, Apple a Day Crunch Away, 161
Sandwiches, Red Hot Quinoa Burger, 174
Sandwiches, You Get Na'an, 53
Sauce, Tomato, 169
Seasoning, Bayou Shake, 78
Seasoning, Cajun Spice Mix, 167
Seasoning, Taco, 162
Seasonings, Home-Made Chai Mix, 219
Smoothies, Monday Morning Matcha, 175
Smoothies, Strawberry mango, 21
Smoothies, Summer Season, 21
Smoothies, Pumpkin Fall Forward, 21
Smoothies, Ginger Tummy Tonic, 22
Smoothies, Beet It, 22
Smoothies, Add-Ins, 24
Smoothies, Cool Breeze, 147
Smoothies, Banana Cranberry, 161
Smoothies, Peaches & Ginger Cream, 178

Snacks, Skinny Dip & Pita Chips, 175
Soup, Chicken Taco, 94
Stew, Trouble, 93
Stew, Beef, Island, 149
Stew, Lentil Bits of Love, 179
Stew, Da Yard Beef, 92
Stout, Stamina, 218
Substitutes, 197-199
Sweets, Celebration Mango Mousse, 216
Sweets, Ginger Coconut Drops, 214

T
Tea, Lemongrass Iced Tea, 218
Tomato, Sauce, 169
Toppings, He's Fakin Bacon, 116
Turkey, Meatloaf, 77

V
Veg, Tex Mex Zucchini w/Black Bean Guacamole, 110
Veg, Sautéed Beans & Zucchini, 111
Veg, Kale Fritters, 112
Veg, Chick Peas & Curry Run Down, 113
Veg, Shakin That Buddha Bowl, 119
Veg, Spicy Q'd Corn on the Cob, 120
Veg, Guacamole, Fried, 123
Veg, Cabbage & Corn, 124
Veg, Soul Good Sushi Rolls, 164
Veg, Rascallion Pancakes, 177
Veg, Muah for Quinoa, 182
Veg, Quinoa Burrito Bowl, 183
Veg, Hurry Curry, 184
Veg, Banana, Fritters, 131
Veg, Drunken Over It Beans, 97
Veg, Black Eyed Pea Fritters, 98
Veg, Black Bean Stew, 103
Veg, Moody Chick Peas, 127
Veg, Real Loaf, 185
Veg, Quinoa Chick Burgers, 125
Veg, Apple a Day Crunch Away, 161
Veg, Red Hot Quinoa Burger, 174
Vegan Carrot Dogs, 55
Vegan, Crispy Tenderonies, 117

Vegan, No Yo Mayo, 62
Vegan, Vegan Ranch, 62
Vegan, Nacho Usual Vegan Cheese, 63
Vegan, OH BOY NO SOY, cream cheese, 165
Vegan, Pop Choy, 186
Vegan, Scrambled Vegan Eggs, 181
Veggie, Jerk, 72
Veggie, Ital Patties, 99
Veggie, Herb Bake, 102

## W
Walnuts, Candied, 209
Wine, This is Bananas Wine, 217

## Z
Zucchini, Sautéed Beans, 111
Zucchini, Tex-Mex w/ Black Bean Guacamole, 110

## FOOD FOR THOUGHT

I would like to see people read this book and have enough courage to invite people into their homes to be fed. People who don't look like them, people who don't roll like them, people who have different life experiences, different bank accounts, people whose complexion may be different than theirs-fear makes people keep themselves apart from each other. I want to see ordinary people have an extraordinary conversation with everyday people. SPEAK! SHARE! Eat fudge, don't judge! Strike up a conversation, be courteous, take time to laugh at ourselves and lift someone up. Be mindful of how you eat & how you relate. Be intentional to care for yourself & others, and pay attention to how both affect your body. Introduce consideration back into our lives; into our homes, our kitchens, our living rooms, and our class rooms.

~W. Kay Wilson